Where the Dream all began.
— Jim

THE AMERICAN DREAM

How the Free-Market
Economy Is Eroding It
And What We Can
Do to Restore It

James V. Cammisa, Jr.

**THE
AMERICAN DREAM
BOOK SERIES**

Copyright © 2011 James V. Cammisa Jr.
All rights reserved.

ISBN: 1463526113
ISBN-13: 9781463526115

Library of Congress Control Number: 2011911314

Dedicated to the Memory of
Commander James J. Cammisa, M.D.
United States Navy Retired

*My Father, an Immigrant Who
Lived the American Dream*

CONTENTS

Preface

INTRODUCTION 1

PART I – THE AMERICAN DREAM 5
 1. The Dream and Its Meaning 7
 2. How the Dream Evolved 19
 3. The Golden Age of the Dream 43

PART II – THE EROSION OF THE DREAM 55
 4. Impact of the Free-Market Economy 57
 5. Rising Levels of Financial Anxiety 83

PART III – RESTORING THE DREAM 93
 6. The Role of Social Safety Nets 95
 7. Restoration Agenda and Responsibilities 127

CONCLUSION 147

Author Postscript *153*
Appendix *157*
Data and Statistical Sources *203*
Bibliography *205*
Acknowledgements *211*

Preface

The research and writing of this book took place at my retirement home in Florida. As most everyone knows, retirees reminisce a lot – going back over the years and rehashing their most memorable experiences. That's what started me to think about writing this book.

In retracing my college days, now more than fifty years ago, I decided to re-read some of the books that had then appeared on my course reading lists. Like many students looking for shortcuts, I had only skim-read many of these books. Now I would read them from cover to cover. As an American history major at Harvard College in the 1950s, I had the good fortune of having an outstanding faculty and scholars who were also prolific writers. These included Samuel Eliot Morison, a colonial and maritime historian; Oscar Handlin, an immigration expert; Frederick Merk, an authority on the nation's westward expansion; and, the father and son team of Arthur M. Schlesinger, Senior and Junior. Most everyone in this group was a Pulitzer Prize winner. Re-reading the books of these authors renewed my interest in American history, and led me to think about what became known as the American Dream.

The second influence and reason for this book is that I'm the son of immigrant Italian parents who lived and shared the American Dream with me as I grew up in the post World War II era. I attended the nation's oldest public school, founded by the Puritans in 1635. It was the Boston Latin School. Like me in the 1950s, a large portion of the student body was first- generation Americans – the sons of Irish, Italian, Greek, and Jewish immigrants who came to our country at the turn of the 20th century. The school had a tough, classical curriculum, and was a so-called "gateway school," with most every student going on to college. From my class, Harvard accepted forty-eight of us. Passing through this gateway gave us all an opportunity to succeed in life, to do better than our parents, to lead a fuller, richer life. That is what the American Dream is all about.

Working on this book has become one of the highlights of my retirement years, for another and final reason. I have six grandchildren, and as they mature, I want to see the American Dream stay alive for both them and for the generations that follow them.

Bal Harbour, Florida
September 2011   James V. Cammisa, Jr.

Introduction

More than 350 years ago, the seeds of a new nation were planted here on our shores by a few hundred Englishmen and their families. They were not adventurers, hunters or traders, but families in search of a better life for themselves and their children. Over time, thousands more would arrive, settling in thirteen Atlantic coast colonies.

On July 4, 1776, the colonies became a new nation. In the decades to follow, these settlers, as well as new arrivals, saw their nation grow and prosper. What started as a dream for them would now become a reality. America was indeed proving to be a land of opportunity, with an endless supply of land, a nation where one could achieve a better, richer, and happier life, where every individual had an equal chance of rising from rags to riches. One would have to work hard, but there were rewards at the end of the journey – not just financial rewards, but a better life. These opportunities and the values associated with them are what we know as the American Dream.

In the chapters that follow, we will see that the American Dream is not a doctrine or a set of principles codified in legal documents. Rather, it is a cultural ideal, a set of attitudes and beliefs unique to this country. Social scientists tell us that culture

The American Dream

counts, and it may very well explain our nation's achievements and successes over the course of its history.

This book begins by defining the meaning of the American Dream for our readers. This is followed by an historical perspective that focuses on those periods and events in our nation's history that had the most significance in shaping the Dream. The perspective begins with the birth of the Dream in the early Puritan settlements established in New England. We then examine the role of the Founding Fathers in formulating the ideas that are an integral part of the Dream. The importance of the frontier society, America's westward expansion, and the rise of the common man are discussed, and tell us more about how our national character was molded. And, finally, we look at the new dimensions that the waves of immigration added to the Dream at the turn of the twentieth century.

In our historical examination, we will meet some of the personalities and icons who did the most to build the Dream as we know it today. These icons were not just statesman, but from diverse fields that included social activists, writers, artists, and even entertainers.

Do all dreams come to an end? Hopefully not this one. But, without most of us realizing it, there are forces outside our control that have emerged and are now eroding the Dream. Most of these forces are a product of the new free-market economy. They include the deregulation of major industries, economic shocks, the decline of labor unions, offshoring of jobs, and globalization. The book examines these and other free-market forces that are still unfolding and undermining the hopes and aspirations of millions of Americans who believed in the Dream.

The final portion of the book addresses the important need to restore the Dream, and how this might be done. We examine the role that so-called social safety nets can play in helping sustain the Dream in times of difficulty; how they can shield us from the risks and uncertainties that create financial anxiety for everyday families. European social capitalism is examined, and the social safety nets that are used there to provide job stability for working families, educational opportunities for their children, universal healthcare, and secure retirement years. These are what I believe are the four safety net essentials that are needed to cushion the shocks of unfettered free-market capitalism, and in so doing, preserve the American Dream.

Responsibilities for restoring and preserving the Dream are not those of the government alone. I point out that the task requires a three-way partnership between government, businesses, and all of us as individuals. The final chapter of the book defines the role of each party and what each must do, if we want tomorrow's America to truly reflect the promises of the Dream.

The American Dream

It is my hope that readers come away with a better understanding of what became America's cultural foundation – a foundation on which a thriving nation was built. This foundation is now in serious need of repair, and if we don't fix it, everything built above it will fall to the ground.

PART I

THE AMERICAN DREAM

The Dream and Its Meaning
How the Dream Evolved
The Golden Age of the Dream

CHAPTER 1

The American Dream and Its Meaning

"You see things, and you say 'Why?' But, I dream things that never were; and I say, Why not?"

- George Bernard Shaw

Our story begins with a classroom situation that might take place today on any college campus. A world history seminar is underway. It's the end of the semester and the instructor wants to know what the class has learned from the course. Not details by country, but the overriding lessons gathered from the study of many different nations and their history over time.

The instructor begins by posing a series of questions to the class: What are the factors that determine the survival, success, or failure of nations? Why do some nations prosper more than others? What factors are most and least important in contributing to a nation's economic well-being? Its quality of life?

The American Dream

Back-and-forth discussion then begins among the students and their instructor. One student suggests that God-given factors are the real drivers of a nation's success – its geographic location, its climate, and its natural resources. Another student, a business major, cites economic strengths and weaknesses – a nation's industrial output, the quality of its workforce. Several students bring us the role of government – the type of government, its political parties, legislative accomplishments, and the capabilities of its leaders. Then, a student known for brevity and impatience, tries to dismiss the need for a lengthy discussion on the questions before them. He cites his recent readings on country rankings given to individual nations by such non-partisan international organizations as the United Nations and the International Monetary Fund. Each of these organizations, he says, constructs statistical rankings, based on such measures as per-capita gross domestic product, industrial production, employment, and unemployment. He points out that they also develop so-called "quality of life" measures reporting life expectancy, school enrollment levels, and leisure time availability. One only needs to look at the national rankings, he says, to answer the questions raised in the classroom discussion. Perhaps he is right. Many believe that everything in life can be reduced to a set of numbers.

In the instructor's semester-long course, and in this final session, unfortunately there was no discussion of the role that a country's national culture plays in how it will rank among the nations of the world. A national culture? What is that all about? Isn't it something that is taught in a cultural anthropology class? You remember: Margaret Mead, Ruth Benedict, and others, who studied the importance of ancient and modern cultures in different countries around the world. These scholars defined national cultures as:

> A common set of shared ideals, attitudes, assumptions, and values that have grown and endured over time, and have influenced the way a nation's people think about themselves and their country.

In their studies, anthropologists describe what they termed strong and weak cultures, those characterized by a work ethic, and others with slovenly attitudes toward work; innovative entrepreneurial societies versus those who were just followers. Scholars admit that culture is something that is hard to measure or quantify. It's part economic, part psychological and, therefore, characterized by complexity. But it's what they believe makes some nations outperform others. A unique culture is what many believe makes our nation distinctive and one of the leaders in the world. This culture has been termed the American Dream, and the focus of our book.

The American Dream

The use of the phrase, The American Dream, is credited to James Truslow Adams, an historian who, in 1931, published a book entitled, *The Epic of America*. Adams was a colonial historian. He published books on the New England colonies as well as works on Jefferson, Adams, and Hamilton, three of the nation's Founding Fathers. *The Epic of America* dealt with historical events and issues that the author believed had a bearing on the shaping of the American character. In the book's concluding chapter, Adams defined what he saw as The American Dream:

> The dream of a land in which life should be better and richer and fuller for every man, with opportunity for each according to his ability or achievement ... It is not a dream of motor cars and high wages merely, but a dream of social order in which each man and each woman shall be able to attain to the fullest stature of which they are innately capable, and to be recognized by others for what they are, regardless of the fortuitous circumstances of birth or position.

The first and most comprehensive analysis of Adams' work was done in 2003 by Jim Cullen, a writer and professor of American Civilization. In an excellent book, *The American Dream: A Short History of an Idea that Shaped a Nation*, he explored the multifaceted dimensions of the Dream, including equality and upward mobility and how they molded the American character.

In its original use, and later on, when examined by others, the Dream was not seen as a political, economic or social doctrine. Rather, it was a cultural ideal, an aspiration, a national ethos or credo. It is the common set of ideals, attitudes, values, and beliefs that cultural historians say have influenced the way Americans see themselves and their nation. The Dream has other underlying principles – the sense of possibility, high expectations, and personal fulfillment – that by working hard and doing the right thing anyone can succeed in this country of ours. It's a "can-do" attitude characterized by optimism and hope about the future. One of these hopes, and what became beliefs, is that our children will do even better than we do – becoming better educated and able to take advantage of living in an upwardly-mobile society. Yes, it's true, our country was blessed with bountiful national resources, but it took an American work ethic to reap its benefits. New industries were built by Americans who were willing to innovate and take risks. These multi-faceted cultural attributes were the driving force behind the social, political, and economic accomplishments of our country.

Over the years, scholars have used a series of descriptive phrases for us to better understand the characteristics that are an integral part of the Dream. Seymour Martin Lipset, a noted university professor, cites five: liberty, egalitarianism, individualism, populism, and laissez-faire. Lawrence E. Harrison, who has written a number of books on national cultures, cites what he calls eight values that describe the American national culture: freedom, justice, work, education, excellence, frugality, family, and community. A number of Calvinist values are seen by scholars to be an important part of our culture: self-reliance, enterprise, hard work, austerity, and obligations to one's community. Though these are religious tenets, they are seen to also apply to America's secular culture.

Sometimes, the best insight into our country's culture comes from the observations of foreigners such as Alexis de Tocqueville, Frances Trollope, and even Charles Dickens. The most widely respected and quoted observations are those from Tocqueville. He was a French aristocrat whose government sent him to the United States in 1831 to study our prison system. He spent nine months here, traveling extensively through our cities and into the hinterland. His research on prison systems became secondary to what he would analyze and write about in a magnum opus, published in two volumes in 1835 and 1840. Titled, *Democracy in America,* it is still in print, and widely quoted and considered essential reading at our colleges and universities.

The American Dream and Its Meaning

Tocqueville saw distinctive, and in many cases exceptional characteristics in the American culture that had been formed in the two-hundred years following the Puritan settlements, and more than fifty years after the formation of our nation. Here's a short sampling of his observations that relate most closely to the American Dream. On equality, he wrote:

> Amongst the novel objects that attracted my attention ... in the United States, nothing struck me more forcibly than the general equality of condition among the people ... The more I advanced in the study of American society, the more I perceived that this equality of condition is the fundamental fact from which all others seem to be derived.

On the work ethic of Americans, he pointed out:

> Among a democratic people, where there is no heredity or wealth, every man works to earn a living ... Labor is held in honor, the prejudice is not against it but in its favor.

And, on upward mobility, again his comments were insightful:

> When all the privileges of birth and fortune are abolished, when all professions are acces-

sible to all, and a man's own energies may place him at the top of any one of them, an easy and unbounded career seems open to his ambition, and he will readily persuade him that he is born to no common destinies.

One of the keenest observers of our culture, and the values it should possess, was our own American icon Benjamin Franklin. This eighteenth-century son of a candle-maker became a printer's apprentice, moved to Philadelphia and, as they say, the rest is history – successful businessman, scientist, author, diplomat, and one of our Founding Fathers. His writings left us with dozens of well-known aphorisms, many of which focused on the multiple dimensions of the work ethic and frugality. Here are just a few that most of us have heard:

- Diligence is the mother of good work.
- A penny saved is a penny earned.
- An interest in knowledge always pays the best interest.
- Honesty is the best policy.
- Beware of little expenses. A small leak will sink a great ship.

Americans celebrate their heroes and icons with monuments and statues, and by embossing their names on public buildings. Their faces appear on our currency and postage stamps. For the most prominent, there are national holidays. Who are these icons? There is no official designating organization, and different points of view exist among historians as to who should and should not be included. What follows is our own list.

The criteria for being included are that their lives symbolized the American Dream either through accomplishments, personal characteristics, or legends associated with them. In the latter category some might even include the actor John Wayne, whose image as an American hero was built through his fictional film roles in westerns and war movies. His admirers in California named their Orange County Airport after him when he died in 1979.

The Founding Fathers are an obvious first group of icons. There were seven: George Washington, John Adams, Thomas Jefferson, James Madison, Alexander Hamilton, John Jay, and Benjamin Franklin.

A second group of importance is a select list of U.S. presidents. These include Abraham Lincoln, Theodore Roosevelt, and Franklin Roosevelt. Each are usually named highest in presidential rating surveys conducted by historians. John F. Kennedy also can be considered an icon, not necessarily for the accomplishments in his brief term in office, but rather for the images associated with him – courage, youthful energy, and a sense of possibility. In his 1960 inauguration speech, he spoke of "standing on the edge of a New Frontier – one of unfilled hopes and dreams."

Adventurers and pioneers are another icon category. Frontiersman Daniel Boone was one of the nation's earliest common-man heroes, as he boldly ventured beyond the borders of the thirteen colonies into the western wilderness. Davy Crockett was another whose mythical deeds, popularized later on, probably exceed his real life accomplishments. In the twentieth century, a different kind of pioneering national icon emerged – a twenty-five-year-old airmail pilot, who, in May of 1927, made the first non-stop transatlantic flight, piloting his Spirit of St. Louis from New York to Paris. Hailed as an American hero, Charles A. Lindberg was awarded the Medal of Honor. The last pioneer in this group of icons is Neil Armstrong, the astronaut who was the first to set foot on the moon in July of 1969, as part of the Apollo 11 space program. The latter two individuals became symbols of the "can-do," "anything is possible," characteristics implicit in the Dream.

Literary and art figures made important contributions in interpreting the Dream for the public. For many, Mark Twain is considered to be the father of American literature, with his novels depicting everyday American life. Readers in the same period in the nineteenth century also read essayist and poet Walt Whitman, best known for his collection of poems in the *Leaves of Grass*. He was considered to be "America's poet," with one literacy critic saying, "if you are an American, then Walt Whitman is your imaginative father and mother." Beyond the contributions of these literary figures were those of the twentieth-century painter and illustrator Norman Rockwell, with his depiction of everyday American life and values, popularized in the magazine *The Saturday Evening Post*. His most famous paintings were inspired by a Franklin Roosevelt speech in which the president introduced us to his Four Freedoms. In 1943, Rockwell did a series of Four Freedom paintings for the magazine, all of which are now considered national treasures: Freedom of Speech, Freedom of Worship, Freedom from Want, and Freedom from Fear. Social activists should also be included in our list of icons. Foremost among these is Martin Luther King, Jr., whose contribution to the American Dream is discussed in a later chapter. He has been honored with a national holiday in his name, enacted by President Ronald Reagan in 1983.

A final category of icons is that from the entertainment industry, whose members have always enjoyed the benefits of high visibility among the American public. Our list starts with Will Rogers, one of the country's most admired twentieth-century humorists, with a folksy style and common-sense observations on American life. His beginnings were humble and, true to the American way, he made it to the top of his profession. Another twentieth-century icon is one of the fathers of American Musical Theater, George Gershwin. As a leading composer, he wrote scores for dozens of hit Broadway shows and Hollywood films. In the same era, George M. Cohan came into prominence as a playwright, composer, and lyricist. His most popular songs were patriotic ones – *Over There*, *The Yankee Doodle Boy* and *You're a Grand Old Flag*. And, finally, there was Irving Berlin, who wrote what is considered the nation's second national anthem, *God Bless America*.

There are obviously others that our readers can think of. But what distinguishes those we have mentioned is that their reputation and legacy has lasted long after their deaths. In spite of very different backgrounds, each in his own way became lasting symbols of the American Dream.

In this opening chapter, we have introduced our readers to the Dream concept – how the phrase was first used and what it means. The next chapter will provide a deeper understanding of how the Dream has evolved over time. Each new generation has added something to it, and we will look at what those additions and reinforcements have been. The Dream is still alive, but as we will see later on, the twenty-first century has brought with it new developments that threaten to erode it.

CHAPTER 2

How the Dream Evolved

"An Englishman is a person who does things because they have been done before. An American is a person who does things because they haven't been done before."
- Mark Twain

In the previous chapter we discussed the work done by social scientists on the study of national cultures. Their work helps us better understand the concept of the American Dream, and the ideals, attitudes, and values associated with it. What these scholars also tell us is that national cultures are not static, but evolve over time. The individual characteristics of a national culture may either grow or decline in importance as changes occur in a nation's demographics, its economy, government, and social institutions. Scholars also point out that, in spite of such changes, the true test of a national culture's strength lies in its endurance.

In the case of the American Dream, it has both evolved and endured over time. In this chapter,

The American Dream

we will look at five influential building blocks that have shaped and strengthened the Dream over the course of our nation's history.

Puritan Ideals

Every school child knows that the first permanent settlements in America occurred in 1607 at Jamestown, Virginia. There were one hundred, five settlers. Next came those in Massachusetts, starting with the Pilgrims landing at Plymouth Rock in December of 1620. There were one hundred, two hearty souls who made the ocean crossing on the Mayflower. The third and most significant settlements, in terms of the real birth of the American Dream, came in 1630, with John Winthrop's Massachusetts Bay Company. An English barrister and religious reformer, he organized a fleet of ships with nine hundred individuals sailing from England in April 1630. His settlements were established in a series of towns along the shores of what is now known as Boston Harbor. Winthrop would serve as the company's leader for most of the next twenty years. During that time, the settlements would grow to more than 25,000.

The new settlers were not explorers, adventurers, or traders, but rather families separating from their church in England to seek a better life in a new and distant land. They called themselves Puritans. They believed that a better life was possible for both themselves and the church. This was the essence of the American Dream, and that dream had now begun.

Hard work would be necessary for this dream to be fulfilled. Geography was not in the Puritan's favor. Unlike the Jamestown settlement, New England soil is of glacial origin and short summers made raising crops difficult. The settlers would have to look to the forests, rivers, and streams as resources from which they could build their colonial economy. Fishing, hunting, and shipbuilding therefore quickly became important local industries. Of necessity, individual entrepreneurs made up a large portion of the workforce – tanners, blacksmiths, masons, wheelwrights, glazers, and millers. Common to all these occupations was the presence of a work ethic that later scholars would cite as an integral part of the American Dream. The Puritans believed that self-discipline and hard work was their calling – not for a better life in the hereafter, but on Earth today.

The Puritans had strong beliefs about the importance of education, as they saw literacy as necessary in order to possess knowledge of the Scriptures. The city of Boston established the first town-supported public school, the Boston Latin School, in 1635, just five years after the Puritan arrival in America. A decade later, every town in Massachusetts with fifty households or more was required to hire a teacher; those with a hundred or more households, had to establish a grammar school, as well. Educational opportunities for everyone became part of the American Dream.

The Puritans believed that the new society they were going to create would be a model for others. Prior to their landing, and on board John Winthrop's flagship, *The Arabella,* he gave his famous "City Upon a Hill" sermon that proclaimed: "For we must consider that we shall be as a city upon a hill the eyes of all peoples are upon us." The "City Upon a Hill" theme has been used continually over the years, most recently by John F. Kennedy and Ronald Reagan.

It may surprise many to know that, in the opinion of many, it was the religious teachings practiced by the Puritans that contributed most to their ability to build a successful new world society. The Puritans believed in separation of church and state, and this as we know, is one of the foundations of a democracy. They believed in egalitarianism, as can be seen in the importance they gave to active parishioner participation in religious ceremonies and church matters. The congregation was important. This is in contrast to the top-down hierarchal structure of the then prevailing Protestant and Catholic churches that they left behind in Europe. The congregation would later become the model for the well-known New England town meeting, where every citizen enjoyed freedom of speech – later cited by Franklin Roosevelt as one of America's Four Freedoms.

The economic accomplishments of the Puritans and their religious roots have been examined by a number of scholars. In 1904, the German sociologist, Max Weber, published a landmark essay the *Protestant Ethic and the Spirit of Capitalism.* Among the many cultures he studied, he cites the Protestant values of the Puritans as fundamental to economic growth and success of capitalism. The most important of these values was mentioned earlier, a work ethic – the belief that hard work, together with honesty and integrity, were essential responsibilities of the individual in living a good life. It is interesting that, today, Americans are still known for their work ethic, reflected in the fact that we work longer and harder than any nation on earth, even the Japanese.

Over the years, there has been a lot of criticism of the Puritans and their beliefs. Yes, they were in some respects fanatical, uncompromising, and stubborn. The Salem Witch Trials in 1692 are cited as an example of their fanaticism. In spite of this criticism, what they did leave us with is a set of beliefs, values, and standards that were the beginnings of the American Dream.

The Declaration of Independence

Let's now fast forward to a second set of American Dream building blocks. It occurred with the signing of the Declaration of Independence almost one hundred, fifty years after the arrival of the Puritans.

The American Dream

Historian Jim Cullen, whom we mentioned earlier, called the document "the charter of the American Dream." Drafted largely by Thomas Jefferson, it was signed on July 4, 1776, by fifty-six delegates to the Continental Congress. In the opening phrases of the second paragraph is one of the most widely-quoted statements relating to individual rights.

> "We hold these Truths to be self-evident, that all Men are created equal, that they are endowed by their Creator with certain unalienable rights that among them are Life, Liberty, and the Pursuit of happiness."

Like in so many historical documents, concepts and even phrasing are taken from previously published works. The seventeenth-century writings of English philosopher John Locke were one set of influences here. Thomas Jefferson, a Virginian, is also thought to have used the Virginia Declaration of Rights, published prior to the U.S. Declaration, as a source of material. The Virginia document had been drafted by George Mason, a fellow Virginia statesman. Today, a 32,000-student university in Virginia bears his name. The phrasing used by Mason was:

> "The enjoyment of life and liberty, with the means of acquiring and possessing property, and pursuing and offering happiness and safety.

Significant is Mason's inclusion of phrases relating to property rights, not included in the U.S. text. Jefferson evidently did not see economic well-being as an essential and unalienable right. Both the Virginia and U.S. documents include the rights relating to happiness – one of the important non-economic components of the American Dream. Today, it is getting a good deal of attention from many who believe that our country has relied too much on economic success to measure progress and the public's well-being. Rather than using Gross Domestic Product (GDP) as a metric, researchers are now trying to develop measures of what they term "Gross National Happiness (GNH)." The research is being funded by non-profit organizations. Their goal is to develop statistical "quality of life" measurements that take into account living standards, health, education, leisure, and culture. The Founding Fathers didn't have the benefit of such research, but they had the foresight to know the importance of happiness as an unalienable right.

Over the years, as historians have examined and re-examined every word in the Declaration of Independence. What has gained increased scrutiny is the phrase, "that all men are created equal." What about women? No mention. What about the black slaves still in servitude? No mention.

Equality for women would have to wait many more generations, with serious moves for equal rights not beginning until 1848, when social activist Elizabeth

Cady Stanton organized the first important women's conference in Seneca Falls, New York. There, the group drafted a Declaration of Sentiments, closely patterned after the Declaration of Independence. It dealt with demands for equal rights in marriage, education, religion, employment, and public life. Following this ambitious start, the movement would move forward only slowly. It was not until 1920, with the ratification of the nineteenth Amendment to the Constitution, that women received the right to vote – 144 years after the Declaration of Independence was signed.

For African-Americans, the road to equality would also be a long, difficult one, with the first of many existing barriers to equality not removed until eighty-six years after the Declaration of Independence was signed. The Emancipation Proclamation, in a series of two executive orders, was issued in 1862 and 1863, followed by the Thirteenth Amendment that banned slavery completely; and finally, the Fifteenth Amendment in 1870. The latter amendment declared that "the rights of citizens to vote could not be denied on account of race, color, or previous conditions of servitude."

True equality for African-Americans would still take a good deal longer, and not gain real momentum until the Supreme Court's 1954 Brown vs. the Board of Education ruling ending school segregation. The Civil Rights movement, as we know it today, really began after a seat in the white section of a Montgomery Alabama bus was denied to Rosa Parks. Martin Luther King, Jr., was now on the scene, and his enormous influence would be felt until his death in 1968. King saw the passage of the Civil Rights Act in 1964, banning discrimination in employment practices and accommodations. Then, the Voting Rights Act outlawed a variety of discriminatory voting practices. President Lyndon Johnson spearheaded both.

In spite of these gains during the 1960s, African Americans had much further to go before they could fully share in the American Dream. In one of history's most memorable speeches, Martin Luther King, Jr., expressed his hopes for the future. Standing at the foot of the Lincoln Memorial in Washington on August 28, 1963, before a crowd of 200,000, he gave his famous "I Have a Dream" speech in which he said.

> "In spite of the difficulties and frustrations of the moment, I still have a dream. It's a dream deeply rooted in the American Dream ... that one day this nation will rise up and live out the true meaning of its creed: We hold these truths to be self-evident: that all men are created equal."

On November 4, 2008, Barack Obama was elected the forty-fourth President of the United States. In his victory speech in Grand Park, Illinois, we heard him say:

The American Dream

> "If there is anyone out there who still doubts that America is a place where all things are possible; who still remembers if the dream of our founders is alive in our lives; that still questions the power of our democracy, tonight is yours, America."

Two years earlier as a young senator from Illinois he had written a book entitled: *The Audacity of Hope: Thoughts on Reclaiming the American Dream.*

The pursuit of equality for other minority groups continues today – for Native Americans, Asians, Hispanics, gays, lesbians, and other minorities. The Declaration of Independence was flawed in not dealing with these issues, but it was a different time. The document was, however, one of the important Dream building blocks. Historian Jim Cullen called it the *Magna Carta* of the American Dream.

The Rise of the Common Man

On the fiftieth anniversary of the signing of The Declaration of Independence, an unusual historical coincidence occurred. The date was July 4, 1826, when two of the Declaration's most prominent signers died on that same date. Thomas Jefferson passed away at his home in Virginia; John Adams died at his home in Massachusetts.

The deaths of these Founding Fathers marked the end of an era and the beginning of another. The country was moving from an agricultural society, characterized by small freeholder farms, to a commercial and industrial one, where an increasing proportion of the population were wage earners. The landed interests of the earlier era were represented in government by aristocrats. All six presidents, four from Virginia, and two from Massachusetts, had wealth-related or aristocratic backgrounds.

As in most periods of historical change, the circumstances of the time brought forth new and different political leaders. In this case, in 1829, Andrew Jackson would come forth as that leader, championing the rights of the common man. Born to Irish immigrants in a backwoods Tennessee town, he would distinguish himself in military uniform as a courageous Indian fighter and foe of British tyranny. Nicknamed "Old Hickory," for his reported toughness, he fought in both the Revolutionary War and the War of 1812. His overwhelming victory at the Battle of New Orleans in 1815 was the last battle of that war, and is considered to be the most dramatic of the war and an important milestone in Jackson's life.

Jackson's military accomplishments, and some of the myth that went with them, were the factors that got him elected to the presidency in 1829. His election was heralded as a victory for the common man – the farmers and laborers in America. These groups, for the first time, would be invited to his inauguration. They came in droves, and reportedly the

White House and its lawn were covered in mounds of debris left by the celebrants. Yes, a common, self-made man could succeed in America, and become its president. Let the celebration begin!

Historian, Arthur M. Schlesinger, Jr., in his Pulitzer prize-winning book, *The Age of Jackson,* saw the historical significance of the Jackson administration. While in office, Jackson supported causes that were important to ordinary citizens. His Vice-President, and later his successor, Martin Van Buren, said that Jackson believed "to labor for the good of the masses was a special mission assigned to him by his Creator." Jackson took strong positions against the bankers and was instrumental in broadening voting rights to any white male citizen. Previously, only property owners could vote. During his term, and thereafter, judges would now be elected by the people rather than appointed. Though there were other accomplishments, the symbolism associated with a hardscrabble common man reaching the highest office of the land helped to reinforce the American Dream.

At the time Jackson left office in 1837, there was a twenty-eight-year-old lawyer in Springfield, Illinois, who would become the century's most well-known common man. This was Abraham Lincoln. Born in a one-room log cabin, he was self-educated admitting to no more than eighteen months of formal schooling. As most everyone knows, he rose rapidly in politics, elected to the U.S. Senate in 1854 and the presidency in 1860. What is significant about Lincoln, in the context of the American Dream, is that first he was the quintessential self-made man, and second, an American icon who stood for, and symbolized, the values important in the Dream. His beliefs can be summarized in the closing lines of his famous Gettysburg Address:

> "We here highly resolve that these dead shall not have died in vain. That this nation, under God, shall have a new birth of freedom – and that government of the people, by the people, and for the people, shall not perish from the earth."

The common man, and his role in building our country, would continue, as these individuals and others like them took on the role of pioneers in the country's frontier expansion.

The Frontier

As the common man was building a new set of American ideals, there were exiting new opportunities opening up for those living in the thirteen colonies, as well as new arrivals coming to our shores from Europe. In 1783, as an independent nation, America signed a treaty with Great Britain, formally ending the Revolutionary War and establishing new western boundaries for our nation. That boundary would now stretch westward from the Atlantic Coast (excluding Florida), all the way to the Mississippi River. As the newspaperman, Horace Greely, would say later on, "Go West, Young Man." And Americans did just that.

As we'll see a bit later, the continually moving frontier that characterized nineteenth- century America would have an important influence on shaping our national character, ideals, and values. But first, let's look briefly at how and where this westward expansion took place.

Settlements west, to the Mississippi River, occurred in a number of stages, as Americans crossed the Appalachian Mountains in search of the new opportunities that would come with abundant and inexpensive land. Water transportation would be the primary means of access. The 365-mile Erie Canal was completed in 1825, and feeding into the Great Lakes, helped open the Northwest to settlement. The Ohio River, flowing 1310 miles southwest from Pennsylvania, crossed what are now six Midwestern states. It then fed into the Mississippi River. The Mississippi turned south 2300 miles, terminating in the Gulf of Mexico. Into the areas east of the Mississippi, thousands of new Americans would settle – Germans, in what we now know as Ohio, Wisconsin and Minnesota; Irish laborers working on the rivers, canals, and now railroads; Scandinavians, as farmers in Minnesota, Montana, and the Dakotas. These new arrivals would add a new, multicultural dimension to the American Dream.

How the Dream Evolved

The movement of the frontier beyond the Mississippi River border was made possible by a series of territorial acquisitions that eventually opened the west from the Canadian border to the north, to the Rio Grande south, and all the way west, to the Pacific Ocean. It occurred in three phases. The first was with the Louisiana Purchase from France in 1803. It moved the frontier from the Mississippi River to the Rockies. The second phase came with the acquisition of what we now know as mostly Florida. It was acquired in a treaty with Spain in 1819. The third and final phase occurred between 1845 and 1848, with the annexation of independent Texas; and finally, the Oregon territory, California and the Southwest, the latter rewards from the victory over Mexico in 1848.

The westward expansion, with its moving frontier, is more than a geographic story. Historians and social scientists tell us that it was one of the most important factors contributing to shaping the American character, or as we have defined it – the American Dream. The importance of the frontier was first recognized by noted university professor and historian, Frederick Jackson Turner, who presented a landmark paper in 1893 to the American Historical Association. It was titled, *"The Significance of the Frontier in American History."* Just nine pages in length, Turner set forth his thesis: that the spirit and success of the United States was closely tied to its westward expansion and moving frontiers and that it had defined the American character. He states that, in the West, older institutions fell by the wayside. There were no elite classes. Equality, freedom, and individualism prevailed. Here is one excerpt from his paper:

> "To the frontier the American intellect owes its striking characteristics. The coarseness and strength combined with acuteness and inquisitiveness; that practical, inventive turn of mind; that masterful grasp of material things; that dominant individuallism, working to good or evil, and withal that buoyancy and exuberance which comes with freedom ... America has been another name for opportunity."

Though Turner did not use the phrase, the American Dream, he certainly defined it. He also saw the legacy of the frontier as a lasting one:

> "Long after the frontier period has passed, the conception of society, the ideals and aspirations which it produced, will persist in the minds of the people ..."

In presenting his thesis in 1893, he noted that it was prompted by the fact that in the release of 1890 census data, and by their population movement criteria, the frontier had now closed. It was the end of an era, but in Turner's mind not the end of its significance. How right he was. He lived for forty more years, seeing his thesis become a reality. He must have delighted in reading the twentieth-century western novels of Zane Grey and Owen Wister, fictionalizing his findings.

Through American literature, folklore, theater and films, we still know what riverboats are, trading posts, wagon trains, and the Pony Express. We wear western boots and wide-brimmed hats. Western personalities are still alive and well in our minds – Buffalo Bill, Jesse James, and Billy the Kid. And there also have been modern-day versions of them – Tex Ritter, Roy Rogers, and Gene Autry. The latter, known as "the signing cowboy," became a multi-millionaire in the 1950s as a radio, television, and film star. John Wayne, whom film director John Ford used in numerous western films, stands today as an American icon, a symbol of rugged individualism.

Government played an important role in encouraging settlement of the west and providing the infrastructure needed by the settlers to move westward. Henry Clay was one of their spokesmen. As Speaker of the House of Representatives, and a leading senator over a forty-year career, he pushed his colleagues to support the building of new roads and canals. He understood the needs of the west, and reportedly was the first to view himself and others like him as a "self-made" men.

The most direct government support of the frontier settlers came with the passage of the Homestead Act in 1862. Anyone, including freed slaves, could receive 160 acres of public land from the government, by paying a small registration fee and living on the land for five years. With this Act, a new dimension was added to the American Dream – home ownership.

The Immigrant Experience

Among the many factors contributing to the growth of The American Dream, none was more important than the immigrant experience. Over our country's history, millions emigrated from their homelands, seeking a better life in America for themselves and their children. It wasn't an easy or pleasant experience for these individuals. As one observer put it, the immigrants believed the streets in America were paved with gold. What they didn't know was they would have to pave them.

The immigration process was characterized by extreme personal hardship – leaving one's village, family, and friends, scraping up enough money together for the ocean passage, enduring crowded steerage accommodations, and upon landing, undergoing the watchful scrutiny of custom officers who had the power to deny the immigrant entry into the U.S. That would only be the beginning. The next challenge would be finding a place to live, and a job that would pay enough to support one's family. Most would have to settle for low pay jobs as unskilled laborers.

How the Dream Evolved

How bad did these immigrants want to come to the United States? How important was the Dream to them? The answers to these questions are best told through the experience of individual immigrants, and the stories they in turn told their children and grandchildren. Here's one of those stories, typical of many others, showing the kind of tenacity they would have to have in pursuing the American Dream.

The story is a dramatic one, related by Scott Berg, author of the book *Goldwyn*. It's the year 1879, in Warsaw, Poland, where a Hasidic Jew named Schmuel Gelbfiz is born. He is one of six children, living in an impoverished home. At the age of fifteen, he decides to leave home. Traveling by foot for over a thousand miles, he reaches the coast of France and then makes his way to Birmingham, England, where he has relatives with whom he can live. He stays there for a few years, working at any kind of job to help pay for transatlantic passage to America. He enters the U.S. through Canada, and then takes a menial job as a factory floor sweeper in upstate New York. The ambitious lad rises to sales manager, and a few years later, along with two partners, decides to launch a new career as a filmmaker. He had Americanized his name, and was now known as Sam Goldwyn.

Goldwyn was one of the film industry's founding fathers, starting Paramount Pictures, and later on, Metro-Goldwyn-Mayer. In crossing an entire continent

The American Dream

on foot as a youth in pursuit of a dream, and then as an immigrant, to rise from factory floor sweeper to a leading Hollywood mogul, he had lived the American Dream. Goldwyn received the Presidential Medal of Freedom in 1971 and died three years later at the age of ninety-four.

Historian Oscar Handlin points out that immigrating to the United States went through several distinct phases that began with the Colonial period. The Census of 1790 showed four million foreign-born Europeans, largely English, Welsh, Scotch-Irish, and German. Of these, an estimated half were indentured servants, working here in the colonies to repay debt and gain their freedom. In addition to these, there were nearly one million African-Americans with slavery imposed on them upon their arrival.

A second immigration wave would occur in the early nineteenth century, with an estimated fifteen million arrivals. Half of these were still English, Irish and Scotch-Irish, the balance from other northern European countries including Scandinavia.

A third phase, and the period that gets the most attention from immigration historians, occurred at the turn of the twentieth century – from 1890 to the start of World War I in 1914. This wave of fifteen million was largely now from eastern and southern Europe: Poles, Russians, Jews, Ukrainians, Slovaks, Croatians, Rumanians, Italians, and Greeks. Most of these immigrants settled in fast-growing industrial urban centers. While the earlier generations of immigrants settled the west and built their American Dream there, this last major wave of immigrants built their dream in the cities.

Following World War I, there was a trickle of immigration that then ground to a halt in 1924 with government legislation that set new percentage quotas by country. The quotas favored those from northern Europe, to the disadvantage of prospective immigrants from eastern and southern Europe.

After the worldwide 1930s depression, World War II, and early postwar era, we entered a final phase that opened our doors to immigrants from other parts of the world through the Immigration Act of 1965. As a result, by the year 2000, only 15 percent of foreign-born residents in the U.S. were still of European origin. In 1970, that had been at a high of 60 percent.

The immigrant contribution to our society has been noted by dozens of historians – whether it be business leaders, the sciences and arts, or government. Andrew Carnegie, a Scottish immigrant, almost single-handedly built the steel industry here. He was born in a weaver's one-room cottage in rural Scotland, and came to this country at the age of thirteen. Not only one of America's industrial giants, over this lifetime as a philanthropist he gave charities, foundations, universities and libraries an estimated

$4.3 billion in today's dollars. What America gave him, he gave back in payment for fulfilling his American Dream.

Felix Frankfurter was an Austrian Jewish immigrant who came to our country in 1894 at age twelve. He grew up in a tenement on the Lower East Side of New York City. As an extremely bright young man, he was able to attend college and then graduate from the Harvard Law School. He would eventually be appointed to the Supreme Court by President Roosevelt, and serve on the court with distinction for twenty-three years, supporting many decisions that reinforced the American Dream.

Irving Berlin was a Russian Jewish immigrant, coming to the U.S. at age five in 1898. Throughout the twentieth-century he wrote over 1,500 songs and musical scores for nineteen Broadway shows, and eighteen Hollywood films. At his death in 1989, the *New York Times* obituary told his life story in but a few words: "The classic rags-to-riches story that he never forgot, one that could have happened only in America." A patriot, whose wartime repertoire was extensive, reflected his feeling about his country in the writing of his *God Bless America,* considered America's second national anthem.

In this chapter we have traced the evolution of the American Dream. It was born with the landing of the Puritan settlers in Massachusetts in 1630. Its father was John Winthrop. Then forty-six years later came the Declaration of Independence. The Dream matured in three further stages, with the rise of the common man, the settling of the frontier, and the influence of new waves of immigrants. In each of these stages, new dimensions were added to the Dream, and its basic elements reinforced and strengthened.

CHAPTER 3

The Golden Age of the Dream

"One cannot and must not try to erase the past merely because it does not fit the present."

-Golda Meir

The two previous chapters took us through the early years of the twentieth century when the roots of the American Dream had been planted. As the rest of the century unfolded, there would be some bumps along the road. The Great Depression of the 1930s led many to question whether the Dream could survive. But that decade passed, America went to war, and in 1945, the country stood proudly again. It had fought and won what was termed the "Good War." Good prevailed over evil. We were all proud to be Americans.

The next three decades, from 1945 to 1975, were to become an era of unprecedented prosperity, and a period that represented the golden age for the American Dream. It was not only economic prosperity that contributed to this, but also social and cultural changes. And, in this new era, government would play an important role in fostering the Dream providing social safety nets to prevent its erosion.

American Veterans

August 1945 marked the end of World War II, and the hopeful beginnings of a new life for the sixteen million men and women who served in the nation's armed services. A year earlier, prior to war's end, President Franklin Roosevelt signed the Servicemen's Readjustment Act of 1944, better known as the GI Bill of Rights. Its significance is examined at length in an excellent book by Edward Humes, titled, *Over Here: How the GI Bill Transformed the American Dream.*

If one were to single out specific government legislation over the course of our history that did the most to enhance the American Dream, the GI Bill would be high on the list – right up there with the ten Amendments that made up the Constitution's Bill of Rights, the Homestead Act, and the Civil Rights Act of 1964. Is this an overstatement? Let's examine why it was such landmark legislation.

The GI Bill directly addressed several of the components of the American Dream that were discussed in the previous chapters: education, upward mobility for all, and the dream of owning one's own home. Historians tell us that President Roosevelt saw his legislation as much more than a simple set of benefits due our veterans. He saw the Bill as part of a larger vision – a kind of postwar start toward a new bill of rights – that all Americans were entitled to share in. He had his dreams but, unfortunately, he died only a year after the Bill's enactment.

To qualify for the GI Bill's benefits, one only had to have served in the military for ninety days and receive an honorable discharge. There would be no means testing, nor race, nor gender exclusions. The program was open to every veteran. For college attendance, the Veteran's Administration would pay for up to forty-eight months of enrollment at an educational or vocational institution. The tuition allowance was $500 a year, plus text book payments and a living stipend of $50 to $90 per month, based on marital status. At the time, these payments were more than adequate to cover costs, even at most elite, private universities. Doors were now opened for almost eight million veterans who took advantage of these benefits. By 1947, half of those admitted to our colleges and universities were veterans. When these men and women were originally drafted or enlisted, though 23 percent had high school diplomas, only 3 percent had college degrees. That would all now change. The dream of an education that could open new doors of opportunity became a reality.

Employment assistance was another important part of the Bill. Job placement, as well as a year's unemployment compensation at $20 a week was available.

It was commonly known as the 52/20 Club – and represented a safety net for veterans, while they were looking for employment. In today's dollars, the payment would be the equivalent of $240 a week. Government data show that the benefit was not abused, with the average veteran using it for only eighteen weeks of the fifty-two-week entitlement period.

Home ownership opportunities were another major provision in the bill. The government would co-sign a veteran's mortgage obligation, typically guaranteeing half of one's loan, with interest rates set at a low 4 percent. No down payment was required. Over two million veterans took advantage of these home ownership benefits, satisfying a dream that went back to the Homestead Act of the prior century. Loans for farms and new businesses also qualified for the same kind of government assistance and would help foster the entrepreneurial spirit that we know is part of the Dream.

Though we learned in earlier chapters that the American Dream was characterized by rugged individualism and self-reliance, the success of the GI Bill showed that government could help individuals in realizing their dreams. Individuals would still have to work hard, but their government need not stand on the sidelines, leaving them totally on their own.

Economic Prosperity

As the postwar period began, the United States was the strongest and most powerful nation in the

The Golden Age of the Dream

world. With only 7 percent of the world's population, we controlled half of its manufacturing output. From this base the next thirty years would prove to be the country's most prosperous era. Gross domestic product, adjusted for inflation, more than doubled. Several factors accounted for this high level of growth. There was sizeable pent-up demand for automobiles, homes, furnishings, and appliances. Americans had been deprived of these goods during the Depression years of the 1930s, and they just weren't available in the war years of the early 1940s. Then there was the effect of population growth in creating demand for homes and the goods and services needed by young families. Between 1950 and 1960, the baby-boomer surge boosted the U.S. population by 19 percent.

The absence of foreign competition during the early post-war years was certainly another factor in our growth. War-ravaged Europe and Japan were just beginning to rebuild their economies. Foreign competition in steel, automobiles and shipbuilding was still limited. Finally, there was a technology boom that created whole new industries – electronics, pharmaceuticals, frozen foods, and jet airline travel. And, as many will recall from the 1967 Dustin Hoffman movie, *The Graduate*, the poolside advice given to young Benjamin was simple: "plastics, my boy."

During this post-war period, the standard of living of most Americans rose dramatically. We earned more, ate better, and lived more comfortably than our parents. In just a ten-year period, from 1950 to 1960, median household income, adjusted for inflation, rose by 30 percent. Decade-to-decade income growth of this magnitude has not been seen since then. What was significant is that all income groups shared equally in the prosperity. By 1960, 80 percent of households owned an automobile. Household television penetration was almost universal.

Home ownership, an integral part of the American Dream, surged during these early post-war years. From 1945 to 1955, fifteen million new homes were built, mostly in burgeoning new suburban developments. With mass production techniques used in such new communities as Levittown, home ownership was now affordable for almost everyone. Homes built by Levitt, and others like him, others became picture-perfect symbols of the American Dream. The Levitt built house was a Cape Cod style, four and a-half room home, fully-equipped with appliances, set on a 60' x 100' lot, with shutters and usually a white picket fence. Located thirty miles from New York City, 17,000 of these homes were built. By 1960, on a national basis, 62 percent of families now owned their own homes, up from just 44 percent at the end of World War II.

The rising standards of living that we saw in the postwar period were largely made possible by a growing economy. But, it also came about because businesses and consumers shared equally in the rewards that accompanied this growth. Charles E. Wilson, CEO of General Motors, was much criticized then for his statement, "What's good for General Motors is good for the country." In reality, in that era he was correct. Employers and employees did have a common set of goals and a common set of rewards. There was a social compact between them.

If a corporation's profits grew as a result of the hard work and increased productivity of its employees, wages and salary gains would parallel that growth. Over the period from 1947 to 1973, worker productivity in the U.S. doubled. Median household income was up by a similar amount. The workplace compact was with both a company's blue-collar as well as white-collar employees.

Blue-collar workers had unions working on their behalf, with dynamic leaders such as Walter Reuther, head of the United Automobile Workers (UAW), and George Many, President of the sixteen-million member AFL-CIO. During their tenure, union membership was at its peak, representing a third of all U.S. workers. In 2009, it was down to just 12 percent. The unions pushed hard for and won higher wages, contributions to their pension funds, medical benefits, paid holidays, vacation time, and shorter working hours. Companies went along with their demands, as profits were making the compensation increases affordable. The unions also set the standards for non-union wages and salaries. The blue-collar worker had joined the American middle class and could now share in its dreams. Watching their new television screens in their own homes, they could easily identify with William Bendix, playing the role of a California aircraft factory riveter in the *"Life of Riley."* Peg was his stay-at-home wife. Only one wage earner was needed then in the household. Riley and his family had become members of a new middle class.

For white-collar workers, there was also a social compact with their employers. It wasn't a written one, as in a union agreement, but it was just as real. Author William H. Whyte, Jr., in his 1956 best seller, *The Organization Man*, describes for his readers the nature of the relationship that a typical middle-management employee had with one's company. Whyte's findings and other similar studies show the relationship was usually characterized by job security and benefits, in exchange for hard work and loyalty. One could think of lifetime employment with a company as a real possibility. Salary raises and promotions would come, based on both merit and seniority. Pension benefits were generous by today's standards. In companies with one hundred or more employees, more than 75 percent had defined benefit plans, and these plans were fully funded by the employer with a guaranteed monthly retirement benefit based on the employee's age, length of service, and earnings history. Typically, companies contributed an equivalent 8 percent of the employee's wages to the plans. In 2010, less than a third of companies now have such plans, having substituted 401(k) plans in which employer contributions average less than half those in defined benefit plans.

Role of Government

Throughout the early postwar period, the federal government played an active role in making the Dream accessible to more and more Americans. The GI Bill was noted earlier. The 1950s saw the landmark Brown vs. Board of Education Supreme Court Ruling outlawing "separate but equal" schools. In the next decade, the Civil Rights Act of 1964 became law. In the 1970s, the Equal Rights Commission was created.

The Great Society initiatives of the Johnson administration provided the first meaningful social safety net programs since those of the New Deal. Medicare and Medicaid came into being. Poverty was addressed through the Head Start program for children. And for workers, there was new legislation dealing with workplace health and safety, with the formation of the Occupational Safety and Health Administration (OSHA). Working with the states there were also new and comprehensive unemployment compensation programs to cushion the financial impact of the job losses. What is significant about all these programs beyond their direct benefits for Americans is the fact that they largely were devoid of political partisanship. From 1945-1975, the Republican administrations of Eisenhower, Nixon, and Ford were in office half of those years; Democrats Truman, Kennedy, and Johnson, were in office the other half. Social legislation is normally thought to be the province of Democratic administrations and much of it was. But, it also received the support of Republicans during this period.

Over the span of these thirty years that we have termed the Golden Age, there were, of course, low points – the Korean and Vietnam wars, the assassination of John and Robert Kennedy and Martin Luther King, Jr., the Watergate scandal, and the resignation of a president. But the era's high points outweighed these negatives, with America recovering optimistically from each of the traumas and looking to the future. Prior to his death, John Kennedy, in 1961, told Congress, "This nation should commit itself to achieving the goal, before this decade is out, of landing a man on the moon and returning him safely to Earth." In July of 1969, astronaut Neil Armstrong on the Apollo 11 space mission did just that. Yes, America was a land of endless possibilities.

Though the nation's prosperity would continue into the twenty-first century, there was no period similar to the early post-war years in which so many were able to realize the American Dream in so short a period of time. One of the key lessons learned from this prosperity was that government, businesses, and individuals were partners in its success.

The Golden Age of the Dream

Government's role with the GI Bill and other such programs opened up new opportunities for millions of Americans. Businesses forged a social compact with their employees, sharing in rewards that accompanied prosperity. And everyday citizens did their part - working hard, starting new families, and building a better future for themselves and their children. All three of these partners worked together in creating what we have termed, The Golden Age of the American Dream.

PART II

EROSION OF THE DREAM

Impact of the Free-Market Economy
Rising Levels of Financial Anxiety

CHAPTER 4

Impact of the Free-Market Economy

"The future ain't what it used to be."
-Yogi Berra

The mid 1970s marked the start of another new era for our country, as the postwar boom and the optimism that went with it began to fade. The changes started with a series of severe economic shocks that caused growth to stagnate and erode the well-being of American households. These shocks were followed by the emergence of a new free-market economy that began to manifest itself.

The initial economic shock came in the fall of 1973, when in retaliation for our country's support of Israel, the oil producing nations of the Middle East instituted an embargo of crude oil shipments to the U.S. Oil prices quadrupled, gasoline shortages became common, and industrial output tumbled.

The result was a deep sixteen-month-long recession that lasted through 1975.

Economic distress during this period in the 1970s was also accompanied by other negative developments. Americans were tiring of their Vietnam involvement. The war did not end until 1975. And there was Watergate, with the resignation of President Nixon in the summer of 1974. Beyond these short-term developments and their impact on the economy, there were several broader, longer-term changes that would threaten the sustainability of the Dream. A new free-market economy was gaining hold, brought about by a series of changes that are discussed in the balance of this chapter.

Industry Deregulation

The deregulation of major industries was the first of these free-market developments. Regulation of U.S. industries had gone back to the late nineteenth century. There were several motivations for regulating industries, particularly those that were seen as serving the public interest, such as utilities and transportation. Regulators saw benefits for both the companies and the general public. For companies in industries where sizeable capital investment was necessary, their investments would be protected, with regulators limiting competition and new entrants. But also, since these companies would hold a monopoly position in their industry, there would also have to be an accompanying need to protect consumers from price gouging and inferior service that can occur when monopolies exist.

Regulatory thinking had prevailed in the U.S. until the early 1970s, when fundamental changes were beginning to take place in the economy and the perceived role of government. The Great Society of the 1960s had brought big government – too much perhaps for many. There was also the loss of confidence in government, stemming from the Watergate scandal and the country's prolonged involvement in Vietnam. Free markets and laissez-faire thinking took hold among special interest groups who would gain from more competition and the lower prices that less regulation would bring.

Over the next several years, one-by-one, key U.S. industries were deregulated – in transportation, shipping, rail, bus and the airlines; in energy, electricity and natural gas; in telecommunications, telephone and broadcasting; in financial, banking and the stock brokerage business. What happened to the airline industry was typical of what occurred in these other industries. Passed by Congress in 1978, the Airline Deregulation Act abolished the industry's regulatory body that, for forty years, had set airline fares, granted domestic route authority, limited new entrants, and restricted promotional practices. With deregulation, what followed were intense price competition, fare cutting, new competition on underserved and high-fare domestic routes, a flurry of new entrants, and the expanded use of a variety of promotional incentives commonly used in unregulated industries. The winners in the post-deregulation period were consumers; the losers, were old-line companies that did not change with the times, and unfortunately, the employees who worked the deregulated industries.

In every one of these industries, workers were seriously hurt. As more intense competition took hold, corporate margins shrank and companies were forced to cut costs to maintain their profit margins. New entrants also appeared and used their low costs to offer customers low prices. The obvious target in most cost-cutting programs is employee expense – wages, salaries and benefits. In all the deregulated industries we have noted these actions took place, directly impacting some ten million employees. Millions of other workers were affected indirectly, as lower wages in one industry set new standards in others.

For the economy as a whole, consumer deregulation had positive benefits. But for the millions of those employed in deregulated industries that were laid off or forced to accept lower wages, it was one of several new free-market developments that would work to erode the American Dream.

New Technologies and Automation

Complete books could be written on the impact that new technologies and automation has had on the worlds' economies, businesses, and their workers. Most often cited first is early nineteenth century England, where textile workers rebelled against the mechanization of their weaving looms. Called Luddites, they resisted new technologies which they thought would cost them their jobs. They destroyed the new looms, and, in some cases, whole factories. The government stepped in, arresting, trying, and convicting many of the Luddites.

Over time, we have learned that inventions, innovation, and technology are what drive economic growth, delivering higher levels of worker output at lower costs. We also know that they bring with them labor disruption and displacement. Entire jobs can be eliminated or the number of employees needed to produce the same output can be reduced. And, if the supply of displaced workers then exceeds the remaining jobs available, wages for those still employed can fall. The counter arguments is that, yes, there will be some temporary dislocation, but lower costs of production through automation will (a) result in lower prices for consumers which, in turn, will (b) increase consumer demand, and (c) more workers will therefore have to be hired to satisfy the increased demand.

Beginning in the 1980s, when American industry was forced to compete in a free-market world economy, new technologies that would drive down costs were seen as a competitive necessity. Companies began to see greater returns from investment in

The American Dream

capital rather than in labor. Capital investment in labor-saving devices increased dramatically – not only in manufacturing, but also the services sector. There would be no more bank tellers, telephone operators or secretaries. While robots would replace assembly line employees in factories, self-service computer kiosks would handle banking transactions in the service industries.

The computer and information age was also then upon us. IBM introduced the PC in 1981. The Internet followed a decade later. And, each one of these new technologies spawned dozens of others – e-mail, voice mail, satellite and mobile communications, electronic shopping. Each of these new technologies displaced workers in older industries, but did create new jobs in many newer industries. For example, today, Microsoft has 89,000 employees; Intel, 83,000 employees; Google, 23,000.

Technological progress is not going to stop, and we should not act as the Luddites did. But, what we must recognize is that what will accompany it will be worker displacement and a growing need for retraining in the occupations and skills needed for jobs in newer growth industries. American policy makers have not done very well here as compared to other nations. The extensive occupation apprentice program in Germany is discussed in a later chapter, and perhaps a model for what is now needed in our country.

In terms of the American Dream, we have got to find ways to make new technologies work positively

Impact of the Free-Market Economy

for us to preserve good jobs at good wages, and the upward mobility opportunities that they create. Otherwise, the free-market will destroy the American Dream.

Globalization

Experts have written much about globalization, and the comments here will therefore be brief and limited to its impact on ordinary working Americans and the American Dream.

The basic tenet held by globalization advocates is that, when borders are opened for free trade, there will be more global prosperity. Each nation will pursue what economists call its "comparative advantage." Nations will produce and export what they produce best and import the goods and services that others produce best. Supposedly, every nation will benefit. The more developed nations of the world will import the raw materials they need for manufacturing from the lesser-developed nations. As the exports rise from these poorer nations, their standard of living will also rise and enable them to import high-value goods from the developed nations. In theory, globalization is a "win-win" situation for everyone. In the globalization scenario, multi-national companies also will make plant and equipment investments in other countries. Toyota has five major plants in the U.S. Foreign companies now employ 5.5 million Americans in such plants.

The American Dream

Globalization in many respects was inevitable. The Cold War ended with the fall of the Berlin Wall in 1989. Jet transport freighter fleets enable goods ordered today to be delivered tomorrow in any part of the world. E-mail, the Internet, fiber optic cable, broadband and commercial satellites have erased any communications barriers to doing business globally. And, the world's financial markets are characterized by electronic overnight flows of capital. Beyond these developments, governments have taken action in the elimination of tariffs. They have created free-trade zones and adopted universal free-trade practices developed by such organizations as the World Trade Organization, the World Bank, and the International Monetary Fund.

Globalization has really become America's industrial policy – regardless of the political administration. Our government sees it as being in the public interest by (a) lowering the cost of many goods and services that are imported, (b) encouraging the development in this country of high-value products and services for export, and (c) tapping the export potential in huge markets, such as China and India. Most corporations support globalization as it opens new overseas markets for them. It also enables many to lower their operating costs through outsourcing or offshoring operations to lower-cost wage markets. Globalization proponents argue that any job losses that occur here can be more than offset by the creation of new jobs in high-value industries and employment gains resulting from higher export business.

Impact of the Free-Market Economy

For American workers, it is really another story. It began in the 1980s, when increasing competition from low-cost imports started to impact whole industries and the employees who worked in them – initially, steel, automobiles, auto parts and machinery; then in textiles, furniture, toys and consumer electronics. Many companies in the U.S. were forced to close down completely, downsize, and/or outsource or offshore part or all of their operations to low-wage countries. Blue-collar manufacturing workers have been impacted the most. In 2000, there were 17.3 million employees in the U.S. in the manufacturing sector. By 2007, this had fallen by almost 20 percent.

In the white-collar sector, the erosion began later. Companies have found opportunities to lower wage costs dramatically by outsourcing many of their back-office functions – customer support call centers, accounting, legal, engineering, and administrative jobs. The sharp increase in the size of the educated workforce in the emerging nations has enabled U.S. companies to use highly qualified workers at very low wages and without costly benefits. Chinese universities graduate more than 500,000 engineering students annually. India has a network of seven technology universities and six management schools, graduating thousands each year. What this new talent and wage competition has done is bring about outright losses in American jobs and/or force down the wages and benefits of our workers in many vulnerable occupations. The consulting firm, Forester, estimates that up to

3.4 million white-collar jobs will be outsourced overseas by 2015. Not vulnerable are jobs that require a local physical presence here, e.g., physicians, nurses, teachers, repairmen, beauticians, restaurant employees, and construction workers.

Though there are those who defend globalization, the numbers tell us otherwise. There's a simple scorecard. It's the nation's trade deficit, which is the dollar value of the excess of imports over exports. The figures tell us the value of goods and services produced overseas and imported here, versus those produced in the U.S. and exported abroad. For the pre-recession year 2007, government data show that for every $100 in goods and services we produced and exported to other nations, we imported $130 (the import figures exclude crude oil). The obvious beneficiaries are foreign workers producing those goods and services in their own countries, not our own.

Like it or not, we do live in a borderless world, and that is not going to change. But, far from the hoped-for "win-win" situation for everyone that globalization was to represent, it's at best a "zero-sum game" with both winners and losers. The American worker clearly falls into the latter category.

Decline of Labor Unions

The golden age of the American Dream, described in the previous chapter, was characterized by the strong presence of the nation's labor unions. A third of the workforce was made up of union members. Over the years, they were successful in getting their companies to pay them well, provide job security, improve working conditions, shorten the workweek, and give them excellent health and pension benefits. All of these gains added substance to the American Dream and made it a reality for millions of Americans. The influence of unions was also felt outside their own companies. As a major constituency and voting block, states and the federal government had to be responsive to their needs. These government entities mandated comprehensive workplace safety regulations, unemployment compensation, and worker disability benefits. As broad based government sponsored programs, they would apply to non-union as well as union workers.

Let's fast-forward to 2009 and the Labor Department's annual report on labor unions. Union membership had fallen to a new low of 12.3 percent of the total workforce, with just 15.3 million members. More than half of these were public sector employees. In the private sector, just 7.2 percent of the total force are union members. The peak-to-trough decreases since the 1950s and 1960s have been gradual ones, with a whole host of factors contributing to the declines. Let's quickly highlight the major factors.

Companies in industries that were deregulated in the 1970s and 1980s were all heavily unionized, and in the post-deregulation cost-cutting period, thousands of these jobs were eliminated or replaced by non-union employees. Truck-driver-union membership fell from 60 percent to 25 percent by year 2000; telecommunications workers fell from more than 50 percent to 30 percent. Declines in the manufacturing sector also brought with it sharp reductions in union membership. Factory automation and new technologies had the similar negative effect, with fewer workers needed for the same jobs. By 2009, only 11 percent of employees in the manufacturing sector were union members. Globalization, discussed earlier, is one of the more significant factors in the decline of unions, as it put high-wage union workers in the U.S. in direct competition with low-wage workers in the lesser-developed nations. Guess who won?

As union membership fell, union bargaining power with their companies declined, as did their influence both in state capitals and in Washington. In management-labor negotiations today, give-backs and concessions are a higher priority on the bargaining table agenda than wage and benefit increases. Strikes, which were once a powerful union tool, are no longer a threat at most companies. The landmark event in the demise of the strike occurred in 1981, when President Ronald Regan fired 11,500 air controllers who, as federal employees, were forbidden to strike. They were immediately replaced with supervisors and military controllers who brought the air traffic control system back to normal within a few days. The era of the "replacement worker" was born. Companies became emboldened by Reagan's action and quickly adopted the tactic for their own companies, i.e., "strike if you want, but when the strike ends, there will be no job for you. We have hired a permanent replacement."

What the unions had successfully done in the early postwar years in building the American Dream was now fading before our eyes. Detroit, in the 1960s, was a bustling city with well-paid blue-collar union workers, comfortable in their dream homes on tree-lined streets with manicured lawns. Today, Detroit is only a dream location for journalist metaphors of decay and decline. The captions under accompanying pictures of abandoned homes and neighborhoods usually read, "Is America in Decline?", or "Where Have the Middle-Class Workers Gone?"

Changes in Business Management Practices

As the new decade of the 1980s began, American businesses found themselves operating in a new and difficult environment. The 1981-82 recession was a severe one, the longest and deepest of the post-war downturns. Deregulation in industries mentioned earlier was also underway, and with it, more intense competition in what were once regulated and monopoly industries. And the rising level of imports from abroad was creating new competition for American manufacturers. Profit margins in most every business sector were under severe pressure. There was clearly a need for the nation's businesses to become more efficient, if they wanted to continue to be profitable. Efficiency meant cuts in wages and benefits and getting more work out of fewer employees. That became the new business mantra of the 1980s.

Business literature and new sets of buzz words that came into being gave legitimacy to what were to be out-and-out cost-cutting programs: *downsizing, rightsizing, re-engineering, deleveraging, and benchmarking.* To be respected now in the business community, a company had to be *lean and mean* with its focus on *the bottom line.* Because of the extent of employee layoffs that occurred from these strategies, in 1984 the federal government for the first time began issuing a new monthly mass layoff report showing the number of layoff instances and employee reduction counts – all broken down by industry and area of the country.

New heroes of American business quickly emerged, gaining celebrity status for their success in improving their company's bottom line. One of these was Jack Welch, CEO and Chairman of General Electric. Nicknamed, "Neutron Jack," his relentless focus on operating efficiency won him the *Fortune Magazine* award for the century's best CEO. In his twenty-year career at GE, starting in 1988, the market capitalization of his company soared from $14 billion to $400 billion. In doing this, he became one of the leading poster boys for the concept of "shareholder value."

The concept quickly became another one of the new mantras of the period, and one that still exists today. As defined by most, shareholder value is based on the belief that a company's single most important responsibility is to its shareholders, the company's owners who are entitled to receive the highest returns possible on their stock investment. This would be accomplished through dividend payments, increases in the market price of the stock, and stock buy-back programs. The latter action reduces the number of company shares outstanding and increases earnings per share, which, in turn, can push the share price higher. Though a corporation has multiple constituencies – shareholders, employees, and its customers – it is the shareholders who now count most. Others were so-called "stakeholders," important to American companies, but now of secondary concern.

Wall Street and the growing number of institutional investors quickly embraced the shareholder value concept. When employee layoffs occurred, reducing costs and improving profitability, Wall Street would applaud such actions and the stock prices would rise. So would encouragement for a new breed of corporate raiders and take-over artists whose announced goals would be to "buy or merge companies whose shareholder values could be improved." Nothing, of course, would be said of the financial rewards that would come to the raiders, investment bankers, and their legal firms. In

1987, actor Michael Douglas, playing the role of Gordon Gekko in the movie *Wall Street*, famously told us, "Greed is good." Douglas would win best actor award for his performance as a corporate raider.

Focus on shareholder value triggered another change in business practices that would increase its popularity in corporate boardrooms even further. Company stock awards and options became a preferred means for compensating top executives. If the company's stock rose, these executives could reap sizeable financial rewards. Company management essentially became partners with Wall Street interests.

By the mid 1980s, American businesses were clearly operating in an entirely different manner than in the earlier postwar years. In part, this was of necessity. They had to find ways to compete in the new free-market and in a much more competitive business environment. Others would argue that the new business practices created by a changed environment were one dimensional and were carried a bit far, with injury to the society as a whole. The losers in this environment were the rank and file employees of the large corporations, whose CEOs chose to play by the rule that shareholders come first. The employer-employee compact of earlier years that had been an essential component of the American Dream would no longer exist. Employees would be on their own to sink or swim. Unions would be marginalized, as would white-collar workers. A downward spiral had begun.

New Economy Business Cycles

Economic ups and downs have always been a part of American life. Since World War II, there have been eleven recessions. In these recessions, as demand and production fell, companies would lay off employees but usually rehire them when the recession ended. Though these downturns brought temporary financial harm to employees – largely blue-collar workers – most workers would return to their prior jobs when an economic upturn resumed. Since the year 2000, there have two downturns – the recession of 2000-01, which lasted eight months, and the 2008-09, which lasted eighteen months. The latter was the most severe since the Depression of the 1930s and has been termed, the Great Recession. What has been most significant about the two recent recessions is what occurred in the recovery periods that followed. It was quite different than what happened following earlier downturns. More important, in the context of this book, they both had a direct impact on the endurance of the American Dream.

Loss of Job Security:

The recovery periods following both the 2000-01 and 2008-09 downturns were characterized by what economists now term "jobless recoveries." Companies that made reductions in their payrolls during the downturn replaced only a portion of those who had been laid off and did this much more slowly than in the rehiring period following earlier recessions. Many employees found out for the first time that their temporary layoffs now would be permanent. Surveys of business leaders tell us that during the downturn periods, they learned to live with fewer employees, found ways to get the same output from those fewer employees, used automated equipment and systems, in place of individual workers, or outsourced and sent jobs offshore.

Following the 2001-02 recession, it took three full years for U.S. employment to reach its pre-recession levels. In the 2008-09 recession, a total of 8.5 million jobs were lost. A year after the recession's end, employee counts were rising at only slightly more than what is normally needed to keep up with population and labor-force growth. Government data show that almost half of the unemployed were without work for six months or more, with an estimated five job seekers for every available job. Many economists estimated that the "return to normal" could take three to five years. Americans unemployed or under-employed saw their hopes and dreams for the future downsized. And how about the opportunities for first-time job seekers whose parents had envisioned a better future for them than their own?

Loss of Financial Security:

In the 2008-09 recession, there was both an economic as well as a financial crisis. The credit and financial markets collapsed, and so did the savings and pension accounts for millions of Americans with IRAs, 401(k) retirement plans, and college savings accounts. At the time of the collapse, according to data from the Investment Company Institute, half of retirement plan holdings were in mutual funds and two-thirds of these in stock funds. A full year after the end of the recession, the broad-based Standard & Poor's 500 stock index was still 30 percent below its 2007 level and a similar percentage below where it was a decade earlier.

Home Ownership Losses:

As we have noted in prior chapters, home ownership has always been an integral part of the American Dream – going as far back as the Homestead Act in the nineteenth century. It gave families a sense of security. Perhaps there was a move to a new home to the suburbs, with better schools for their children. Rising steadily in the postwar period, at its peak 69 percent of households owned their own homes. It should be pointed out that the 2008-09 recession was brought on in part because of excesses in these ownership levels, i.e., many who could not afford to own a home were attracted by prevailing low interest rates, easy down payment requirements, and other special inducements promoted by overly-aggressive bankers. What resulted was more home building that eventually created a speculative bubble. It burst in 2006, and was followed by a decline of a third or more in home prices. With price declines of this magnitude, by 2010, one in four homeowners owed more on their mortgage than the home's value. Foreclosures also soared. The loss of one's home and/or the sharp declines in the home's equity struck a blow at what was considered an important part of the American Dream.

Income Stagnation and Inequality

The multiple set of factors present in the new free-market economy, which we have discussed, have worked in combination with one another to bring about a stagnation in incomes for the average household. At the same time that the average American was standing still, those at the top of the income ladder have done quite well. Equality of opportunity was supposed to be part of the American Dream. Household income trends, and where income is concentrated, tell us a different story.

Most of all of the gains made by Middle America in the Golden Age of the Dream have now been erased. Median household income, on an inflation-adjusted basis, in 2010 was actually 8 percent below where it was in 2000. Over the twenty-five-year period, 1980-2005, household median income growth was a mere 16 percent, and this largely came from the increase in the number of dual wage-earner households. The number of married workingwomen with children

Impact of the Free-Market Economy

under eighteen increased by more than 40 percent over the twenty-five year period. If there were to be a remake of the *Life of Riley* television show, mentioned in an earlier chapter, Riley's wife, Peg, could no longer be a stay-at-home wife if she wanted to maintain the family's comfortable middle-class standard of living.

Concentrations of income also have changed in the new free-market economy, with the wealthy seeing their income growth outpace all other groups. Robert H. Frank, a Cornell professor and authority on incomes, points out in his book, *Falling Behind*, that during the period 1949-79, the percent gain in incomes for the top 20 percent of households was essentially equal to the percentage increases for all other groups. That was the period we have called, the Golden Age of the American Dream. A rising tide lifted all boats. In contrast, in the period that followed, from 1979-2003, the top 20 percent saw their incomes mushroom at more than double the rate of increase of all other income groups.

These changes over time have resulted in more and more income inequality – the differences in upper-income household earnings versus that of middle- and lower-income groups. Both economists and social scientists have carefully studied the trends using a variety of measurements. These include statistical measures of the ratio of earnings of upper-income household versus the lowest income groups, or upper-income compared to the median household. Another method is calculation of the changes in concentrations of income among different income groups. Census Bureau data on this measure show, for example, that, in 1970 the top 20 percent of households accounted for 43.3 percent of all income earned by Americans. Yes, these high-income households accounted for a disproportionate share of aggregate income, but more significant is the fact that by, 2009, this figure had risen to 50.3 percent.

For making income inequality comparisons between countries, most economists use what is called the Gini coefficient. Through elaborate statistical analyses, the measure shows the degree to which incomes veer from perfect equality, i.e., every household's earnings are in equal proportion to their size in the population. In a number of Gini-based studies, the findings consistently show the United States with the highest degree of inequality among major industrial nations. Other comparative international studies show similar findings. The Economic Policy Institute, using OECD data for 2007, compared the ratio of median incomes earned by the highest 10 percent to those of the lowest 10 percent. In analyzing figures for sixteen industrial nations, the United States has the most income disparity. Poverty rates are another measure, and here the U.S. is again the loser, with the highest percent of households in poverty – the poverty line here being defined as 50 percent or below median income levels.

As noted earlier, the trends in more income inequality in the United States began in the late 1970s, with the emergence of the new free-market economy. Globalization was a major factor. American workers had to now compete in the international labor market. Downward pressure on low-wage workers resulted, as U.S. companies began outsourcing unskilled jobs – particularly in manufacturing to overseas locations. The well-paying union factory jobs that had for so many been the ticket to the middle class and the American Dream now disappeared. In contrast, premium wages would now be paid to skilled blue-collar and middle-class white-collar workers, widening the gap between low- and high-wage earners. Automation and new technologies were another factor, also discussed earlier, increasing the demand for better educated skilled workers who understood and could work with the new computer-age technologies. They would earn premium wages. Though globalization, automation, and new technological development are now facts of life and cannot be reversed, there are other controllable factors that can be addressed to halt the trends toward more inequality. Businesses reward their top executives with what many see as outlandish compensation. The political power of business lobbyists increases at the expense of the ordinary worker, strengthening the leverage businesses have over their workers.

Inequality is not good for our society. It closes the door to upward mobility. It creates an elite aristocracy living in gated communities and doorman staffed high-rises. None of these characteristics are part of the American Dream.

Consumer Indulgence and Excess

Common to those factors, which have been discussed, was the fact that they were all related to changes in the structural nature of the U.S. economy. They were external factors, largely outside the control of individuals. Consumer advocate groups may have slowed down some of the changes, but for the most part, individuals were powerless in the face of broader-based macro trends.

What the public unknowingly did, however, was contribute to the erosion of the Dream by their own economic behavior in spending beyond their means. As our readers will recall from Chapter 2 of this book, thrift and frugality, practiced by the Puritans, was one of the foundations of the American Dream. It was reinforced by such icons as Ben Franklin, who told us, "A penny saved is a penny earned," and "Be aware of little expenses, a small leak will sink a great ship." Much has been written about consumer excess, materialism and conspicuous consumption, or the latter better known as "keeping up with the Joneses'," and therefore, need no elaborate explanations here. Just a few simple facts tell the story.

In each and every one of the last three decades, starting in the 1980s, consumer spending, on an inflation-adjusted basis, has vastly outpaced the increases in disposable income. The differences between spending and income were financed largely through consumer credit. Over the three decades, credit obligations grew a third faster than income growth. The incidence of savings in the U.S. is reported by the Commerce Department's Bureau of Economic Analysis. It calculates what it calls the "savings rate," which are dollars saved by the public as a percentage of its disposable income. Where, in the early postwar years, the savings rate averaged 6 to 8 percent of disposable income, it fell to nearly zero for most of the last decade. In addition to a low savings rate, the early years of the 2000 decade saw consumers draw sizeable amounts of equity out of their homes – using them as piggybanks. They did this by refinancing their existing mortgages, and in the process, withdrawing equity.

Discretionary spending excess had become the "new normal" of these years. Retailers took pride in their ability to sell "affordable luxury" to "wannabes," which meant getting the middle-market to stretch itself and enjoy the luxuries of the upper classes. Homebuilders built new "McMansions," oversized homes, many of which were elaborately furnished with a high-tech equipped "great room." The homes were financed with a new "jumbo mortgages." Whereas a few decades earlier, "keeping up with the Joneses'" meant striving to become part of the middle class, it had now become an upper class aspiration – whether or not you could afford it.

The American Dream

The 2008-09 recession, the stock market and housing collapse, brought all of this to a halt. Perhaps it was for the better, as consumer surveys now show thrift and frugality may be becoming the new normal for many Americans.

In this chapter, we have discussed eight factors that started the erosion of the American Dream. The golden age of the Dream had ended. The erosion factors were economic ones – the deregulation of major industries, automation and new technologies, the rise of globalization, the decline of labor unions, changes in business management practices, new economy business cycles, income stagnation and inequality, and the excesses on the part of the American consumers. Over time, each of these worked to undermine the individuals' dream of a better life for themselves and their children.

As the so-called New Economy came into being, businesses were forced to break the social compact they had with their employees. Government did the same, with the onset of the Reagan Revolution, whose belief was, "the less government, the better." As has been pointed out in earlier chapters, the three-way partnership – among business, government, and individuals is what had held the Dream together in the past. Yes, our country is characterized by rugged individualism, but if the partnership is dissolved, so too will be the Dream.

CHAPTER 5

Rising Levels of Financial Anxiety

"Anxiety in life is what squeaking and grinding are in machinery that is not oiled."

-Henry Ward Beecher

In the previous chapter, we identified eight free-market economy forces that are eroding the Dream. Millions of Americans have been affected directly by these forces, losing their jobs, seeing their incomes stagnate, and their healthcare and retirement benefits shrink. Beyond those individuals impacted directly, the new free-market economy has had an indirect but significant effect on millions of others. It is a psychological one, best characterized as rising levels of financial anxiety – worries, concerns, uneasiness, stress and apprehension about one's ability to achieve the American Dream. What if I'm laid off from my job? What if someone in our family becomes seriously ill? Will I be able to afford to send my children to college? Will I have enough to live on in my retirement years?

Psychologists tell us that high levels of anxiety can change public attitudes and behavior patterns. Individuals become more pessimistic about the future, less venturesome, and with more aversion to risk. These are not the characteristics that the American Dream was built on. The Puritan settlers and immigrants later on who crossed the Atlantic to a new and unfamiliar continent were risk-takers who had a "can-do," positive attitude on the prospects for themselves and their children.

A number of consumer surveys reflect the anxiety now felt by American households. The 2008-09 recession may have resulted in some overstatement of consumer worries and anxiety, but there's evidence that they are long-lasting ones. The Conference Board, a highly respected non-profit organization, conducts monthly surveys of consumer confidence, asking respondents how they view their financial situation and their outlook for the future. The data show historic lows in the survey readings.

The well-known Pew Research Center conducted a national survey among 2,967 adults a full year after the end of the 2008-09 recession ended and still found lingering uncertainties among the public. Almost half of the respondents were concerned that their financial situation was worse than before the recession, and two-thirds of these expected it to take three years or longer for them to recover. A third said they were not confident they would have enough funds for retirement. In response to questions on their belief that their children would have higher standards of living than they, fewer than half agreed, and 26 percent said their offspring's standard of living would be lower. These responses get to the heart of the American Dream, and the responses were disappointing ones.

In most all of the surveys, there is evidence of households ranking financial security more important to them than greater financial compensation – security against losing one's job, an inability to meet their financial obligations. In a 2009 MetLife Study among 2,240 households, where respondents were asked what the American Dream means to them, two-thirds cited financial security. The absence of adequate social safety nets to protect families from economic shocks and hardship was also highlighted in the MetLife survey. Three in four households felt that they did not have an adequate financial safety net – savings, insurance, or retirement funds. Only slightly more than a third of households were confident that "they will be able to go it alone" – reflecting their uncertainties as to what their employers or government would do to assist them in time of crisis.

Beyond what these attitude surveys tell us about the financial anxiety, there is other hard statistical data that show us that it is real and is increasing. Extensive research has been done on the subject by Jacob B. Hacker, a Yale professor and well-known public policy expert. In conjunction with the Rockefeller Foundation, he publishes what he calls an *Economic Security Index (ESI)*. Using data that goes back to 1985, he has statistical measurements of the proportion of U.S. households whose (a) income has fallen by 25 percent or more in a single year, (b) suffered large out-of-pocket medical expenses, and (c) did not have sufficient funds set aside to deal with the first two risks. In 1985, 12 percent of households experienced these three circumstances, rising to 17 percent in 2002, and estimated at 20 percent in 2009.

If one adds the proportion of households actually experiencing the financial shocks described above, with those who are concerned that they too might suffer similar adversity, the totals would be substantial. Financial anxiety is therefore not a problem for the few, but of high concern among the many. In spite of the public's concern about their ability to "go-it alone," many political leaders still talk of *self-reliance,* a return to *rugged individualism,* an *ownership society, privatizing of social security, empowerment,* and *personal responsibility* – all buzz words for YOYO, or "You are on your own." In the golden era of the American Dream, when the business-government-individual three-way partnership existed, there were shared risks. No one was completely on his or her own.

It is interesting to note that, in every facet of business management, protection against risk is considered a necessity. Companies practice what is called risk management. It is taught in our business schools. Wall Street protects their investors against risks, using short selling, puts, options and futures contracts. Businesses dependent on commodity raw materials execute hedging contracts. Others protect themselves against changes in interest rates or foreign exchange risks. All, in one form or another, are insurance to minimize risk. Such protection can usually be purchased inexpensively because the risks of many are pooled together.

In government, social insurance program risks are dealt with by spreading the costs among rich and poor, young and old, the healthy and the sick. Government can mandate participation and set the premiums for its programs. Government can also encourage business to participate in its programs through incentives, subsidies, and tax breaks. The same kinds of incentives can be used for individual programs, such as retirement IRAs, which are made tax deductible.

What we now see in the first decade of the new century is both a continued erosion of the economic well-being of average Americans, and with it, a rise in the volatility and risks that they face. Financial anxiety has replaced financial security that we once saw in the golden age of the American Dream

Reducing Financial Anxiety

In spite of the fact that anxiety levels for the average American have been rising, little has been done to reduce this anxiety to protect households against the financial risks and calamities they might encounter. Consumers, rather than put aside more savings, have done just the opposite. In the years prior to the 2008-09 downturns, the savings rate had fallen to new lows. Consumers also dug deeply into the equity they had in their homes, withdrawing billions of dollars through refinancing and home-equity loans.

Since 2000, businesses have done little to walk away from their new dedication to profits and shareholder returns, with employees still of secondary concern. The regressive steps taken in the 1980s, continued with less job security for their employees and cutbacks in health and pension benefits. More of life risks have been shifted now by businesses onto the backs of their workers. The government, once a major player in the individual-business-government partnership has stood by the sidelines, doing little to provide stronger safety nets to minimize the higher risks faced by individuals. The thirty-year period, from 1980-2010, saw little in the way of social legislation. Until President Obama took office in 2009, conservative Republican administrations held the seat of power for all but eight of these years. Only the Clinton years saw some social legislation – modest increases in the minimum wage and unemployment benefits and the Family Medical Leave Act. The latter, unlike the paid leave laws in Europe, only mandates unpaid leave for some, but not all workers. Employers with fifty or fewer employees are exempted in the U.S. plan.

The conservative post-Reagan years that began in 1980 essentially ended a twenty-year liberal era that preceded it. Historian Arthur Schlesinger, Jr., tells us in his book, *Cycles of American History* that such swings in the political climate have always existed in American life – periods of public action, social responsibility and concern for the general welfare, followed by periods of laissez-faire, the free-market, and pursuit of profits. He likens the cycles to the "natural swings we see in the tides and the seasons." Changes in political cycles occur, he says, when the public tires of one philosophy or the excesses that may have accompanied it. The twentieth century, he notes, saw the progressiveness of the Theodore Roosevelt and the Woodrow Wilson administrations, followed by the conservative Coolidge/Harding period. Then that ended with the onset of the liberal administrations of Roosevelt and Truman. The post-war years saw a swing back to conservatism and the silent generation of the Eisenhower era. In the 1960s, liberalism re-emerged with the Kennedy/Johnson New Frontier, and the Great Society. In time, Americans then tired of it too. Finally, the pendulum swung again, with the conservative Reagan revolution that we have discussed earlier. Somewhat confusing? Yes, but real. The "cycles of history" concept is probably best explained in Schlesinger's own words

The American Dream

From Conservatism to Liberalism:

"People grow bored with selfish motives and vistas, weary of materialism as the ultimate goal. The vacation from public responsibility replenishes the national energies and recharges the national batteries. People begin to seek meaning in life beyond themselves. They ask not what their country can do for them but what they can do for their country."

From Liberalism to Conservatism:

"Sustained public action is emotionally exhausting. A nation's capacity for high-tension political commitment is limited. Nature insists on a respite. People can no longer gird themselves for heroic effort. They learn to immerse themselves in the privacies of life. Worn out by the constant summons to battle, weary of ceaseless national activity, disillusioned by the results, they seek a new dispensation, an interlude of rest and recuperation."

No one knows at this point in time whether the Obama administration will mark the beginning of another new cycle. The passage of healthcare legislation would suggest it might. On the other hand, we are seeing strong anti-government sentiment among the public – the less government the better, with calls for lower not higher taxes, and cutbacks in entitlement programs as a means of reducing the federal deficit.

Conclusions

In this second part of our book, we have traced how the emergence of the new free-market economy in the 1980s began to take its toll on the American Dream. The process was a slow but significant one that spanned a period of twenty years. As a new decade began in 2000, the erosion accelerated. Between 2000 and 2010, there were two recessions. The second of these was the deepest downturn since the Great Depression of the 1930s. These dual economic shocks, combined with the longer term effects of a free-market economy, have had their greatest impact on the American middle class – not only their economic well-being, but soon their attitudes and outlook about the future. Surveys and changes in consumer behavior patterns all show rising levels of financial anxiety and, with it, questions as to whether the Dream can endure. As the erosion of the Dream began, unfortunately, neither business nor government has wanted to deal with it, standing on the sidelines with the belief that the free-market by itself will self-correct the situation.

PART III

RESTORING THE DREAM

The Role of Social Safety Nets
Restoration Agenda and Responsibilities

CHAPTER 6

The Role of Social Safety Nets

"The welfare of each of us is dependent fundamentally upon the welfare of all of us."
-Theodore Roosevelt

In this final section of our book, we look at ways the American Dream can be restored to what it was and what it should now be – a society in which equality is universal, one in which we expect our children to do better than we did, one in which possibilities are endless. It would be a time when there is an end to the financial anxiety we discussed in the last chapter, an end to unforeseen risks and uncertainty in which one's economic well-being might be destroyed.

Restoring the Dream is more than a moral imperative. It is what built this country, and our nation's preeminence will continue only if the Dream remains alive. Social scientist David Landes and others tell us that it's a nation's culture – above anything else - that determines a nation's success. It follows that, if the Dream is allowed to erode, so will our position as a nation.

Although turning the clock back to the golden age of the American Dream that existed in the early postwar years might be an ideal, it just isn't possible. The world is a much different place. Globalization has changed our nation's economy. New technologies have changed the workplace. All these trends are irreversible.

Some may argue that one way to restore the Dream is to use government more actively as an instrument for absorbing the downside risks that have caused the Dream to erode – guaranteeing employment security, paying for a college education for everyone, providing universal healthcare and worry-free retirement. These are some of the guarantees that European countries provide their citizens. This may be an ideal, but not one that Americans would readily]accept. We are too individualistic and self-reliant. We resist big government, the mandates and taxes that would be needed to pay for more extensive social programs. But there may be an alternative that should be considered – the selective use of safety nets, to help rebuild the American Dream.

Social Safety Nets

Safety nets can best be defined as social assistance programs sponsored by businesses, government,

The Role of Social Safety Nets

and/or non-profit organizations. They are used to assist both the unfortunate as well as households vulnerable to financial risks and hardship. Safety nets may not have been essential to us prior to the emergency of the free-market economy. But, as has been noted in prior chapters, the new economy suggests a need for a fresh look at what safety nets might do to cushion some of the negative effects that the free-market economy is having on Americans.

In a *Washington Post* story in 2007, reporter Steven Pearlstein, quoted excerpts from a speech by Ben Bernanke, the U.S. Federal Reserve Board Chairman. It was a surprising admission by a high government official.

> "One of the reasons the U.S. economy is the most productive and innovative in the world, is that we offer the biggest rewards to skill, effort, and ingenuity. The flip side of this has been to generate not only a higher level of inequality, but also a higher level of economic insecurity. Now, the only way to make these politically acceptable is to put some limits on the downside risks to individuals affected by economic change."

It should be pointed out that the U.S. is not without safety nets. To name just a few, Social Security and Medicare are safety nets for the elderly. The Earned Income Tax Credit, Medicaid, and Food

The American Dream

Stamps, provide support for impoverished households. Unemployment insurance assists displaced workers. And, on the horizon in the U.S., is universal healthcare. Charitable and community organizations, foundations, and other non-profits also provide a variety of programs. The issue at hand, however, is whether in the new environment these current programs are comprehensive enough to help restore the Dream. The most extensive users of social safety nets programs have been the European countries, and though we may not want to mirror what they do, there may be some worthwhile lessons they can provide.

Several years ago, I was invited to speak to a government tourism organization in Finland. With an opportunity to visit a Scandinavian country in a part of the world I probably never would have traveled, I waived my usual speaker's fee in exchange for the group allowing me to bring my wife along, with all expenses paid for both of us. My presentation was well received, with the audience learning something about why and where Americans travel and what Finland could do to attract more visitors from our country. But, what the audience learned was nothing in comparison to what I learned on this visit.

The day following the meeting, the organization assigned a young university professor to give us a tour of the nation's capital city, Helsinki, and discuss any Finnish historical, cultural or social topics of particular interest to us. His name was Jarkko. We spent

The Role of Social Safety Nets

the entire day with our guide. Our day included a long lunch, or what may be better termed a learning session, unlike any I normally experienced. The focus of our discussion was the differences in the American and Finnish societies. Jarkko politely asked whether he could start the discussion with an overview – his observations on what the most significant differences were between our two countries. I can still remember the key points he made.

> It's commonly known, he pointed out, that Finland follows what Americans term *social capitalism.* We are a capitalist nation he said, with a free-market economy, but one that also believes that our citizens are entitled to protection against many of the risks inherent in today's rough-and-tumble world of capitalism, risks that government and businesses can protect them against. This is not to say the Finnish people don't have responsibilities of their own, and that their employers and the government will take care of them – as Americans say, "from cradle-to-grave."

I then asked what he saw as the risks that should be protected against and why he thought they warranted attention and should be part of a nation's public policy agenda. He listed four burdens and risks that individuals face – whether they are rich or poor, young or old. These were (1) education opportunities for all, (2) good, stable jobs, (3) universal healthcare and (4) a worry-free retirement. He saw these as four safety net pillars, each of which we will discuss in more detail later.

As to why these safety nets should be part of a nation's social agenda, our host pointed out that they represented much more than compassion for compassion's sake. They were a means to an end: a more productive, healthy, and economically vital society, one with a high standard of living. The central premise of his "means-to-an-end" argument was that when major burdens and risks are lifted from an individual's shoulders, good things begin to happen. We worry less, we feel freer, and we work harder. Human energy and drive are released, and an environment characterized by entrepreneurship and innovation is created. Free of uncertainties, we enjoy life more. Jarkko noted that, in Europe, vacations are mandated by law, and are six weeks or more, versus the two weeks common in the U.S.

Our host went on to point out that the Finnish society ranks among the highest of nations in both economic and quality-of-life measurements. He suggested that, when I return home, that I check the ratings given to different countries by major international organizations such as the United Nations, World Bank, and others. These include such economic measurements as per-capita GDP, patents per thousand population, research and development expenditures and global competitiveness. The quality-of-life ratings encompass such measures as life expectancy, child well-being, and college enrollment. In total, there were fourteen different indices that I checked, and have updated since then. In eleven of the fourteen, on a worldwide basis, Finland ranked among the top nations. Its median world rank on the entire group of indices was eighth. Quite good for a small nation with a population of just five million.

The accomplishments of the Finns, as well as many other European countries with extensive social welfare programs, counter the prevailing American myth that social welfare programs discourage and inhibit economic growth for individuals and a nation as a whole.

There is a second myth that also exists and one that our host helped us understand. It is that the tax burden needed to pay for social programs is oppressive, reducing the incentive to work and lowering after-tax incomes and standards of living. A number of experts have examined this premise, making calculations of what Europeans pay in income and Value Added Tax (VAT) and what they receive back for those outlays. The first point the experts make is that Americans pay quite a lot more in taxes, much more than is generally believed. Though the average federal income tax rate may not exceed 20 percent, there are FICA and related payroll taxes. Property taxes are another burden. Average U.S. homeowners pay almost three percent of their income to their local community, based on figures compiled by the

Tax Foundation. Though the sum total of these taxes may still fall below what Europeans pay, our taxes are not insignificant.

The second point that analysts make is that Americans must make a sizeable number of out-of-pocket outlays for services that Europeans pay little or nothing for, because they are provided at no cost by their governments. The Kaiser Family Foundation reports that among those American families who have company health insurance plans, the average family's own contribution is now up to $3,900 a year. This expense excludes physician and prescription drug co-pays and, in most cases, dental and vision services.

In virtually every European country, a high school graduate can go on to a state supported college or vocational school, tuition free. In the United States, state college tuition and fees now average $7,000 a year. A family with two children that wants to see each of them graduate from a state school is faced with the need to save $56,000. For a private university this savings requirement would reach $208,000, based on figures compiled by the College Board. All of these exclude the cost of housing and meals.

Retirement savings are another outlay that Americans must make on their own if they want to supplement their very basic social security entitlement. Matching employer-sponsored 401(k) plans and individual IRAs are the vehicles most commonly used, with average workers putting aside a portion of their income. European workers don't have to do this on their own, as their company and/or government pensions are more than adequate to cover their retirement needs.

When all of these out-of-pocket outlays by Americans are added together, many experts say Americans are paying a lot for what Europeans get for free. Following is a partial list of the most common social welfare services found in European countries.

Daycare centers	Unemployment compensation
Job training/retraining	Eldercare
Kiddies' stipends	Retirement pensions
Paid paternal leave	Tuition-free colleges
Paid sick leave	Tuition-free vocational schools
Paid vacations (6 weeks)	

The Four Safety Net Essentials

In the context of these U.S.-European comparisons, let us now look at what the needs of Americans are today in four essential areas that are necessary if the American Dream is to remain alive. They are areas where safety nets can possibly help sustain the Dream. They were the four pillars that our Finnish host discussed.

The American Dream

1. *Educational Opportunities*

In earlier chapters, we've discussed the part that education plays in helping shape the American Dream. The formations of public schools were one of the first and most important actions taken in the Puritan settlements. By 1642, the Massachusetts Bay Colony had made school attendance compulsory. The founding of some of America's great private universities followed within just a few years: Harvard, in 1636 and Yale, in 1701. Publicly funded universities got their start in 1862, with the so-called land-grant colleges. The federal government gave land to the individual states. Iowa State, Michigan, and Penn State were some of the earliest schools to take advantage of the federal grants. The schools were open at no cost to anyone. The emphasis was on degree programs in agriculture, sciences and engineering. In every case, higher education was seen as a key to individual advancement. Immigrant sons and daughters took pride in telling others that they were the first in their families to attend college, and that they had fulfilled their parents' dream for a better life for their children.

The American university system is considered the best in the world – a magnet for foreign students who now fill an increased proportion of enrollments. Our universities are both leaders in academics as well as research. In spite of this preeminence, there is one important flaw: the ability of a sizeable

The Role of Social Safety Nets

portion of young Americans to gain access to and afford the cost of a college education. Data from the College Board for 2010 show the following:

- At public four-year colleges, the annual average cost for tuition, fees, books, and room and board is $23,490. Over a fifteen-year period, costs have more than doubled, rising five times the increase in the Consumer Price Index.
- At private four-year colleges, the average annual cost is $35,640, also more than double what it was fifteen years ago.

The escalation in costs might not be so disturbing if household income growth kept pace with the increases. Not so. Median household income, adjusted for inflation for the comparable period, was up just a mere 8.5 percent. Though those in the top income groups saw higher rates of income growth, the average family did not.

Though the universities maintain that, as their fees have risen, they have been more generous with financial aid. In some cases, this is true. Harvard College charges no tuition or fees to students whose annual family income is below $60,000. This is unusual, and can only be done if the college has a large endowment. The Harvard endowment is $25 billion.

The bulk of student financial aid is not in the form of grants or scholarships, but in student loans. In

2010, a startling figure was released by the Federal Reserve Board. The total amount outstanding in student loans in this country reached $830 billion, an amount equivalent to all of the revolving credit debt owned by Americans on their MasterCard, Visa, and other such credit cards. Never have so few of our young people owed so much to so many of our bankers.

The high cost of a college education has become a deterrent to many qualified high school graduates, and may explain the low world-wide rankings the U.S. has in the percentages of young people enrolled and graduating from college. In terms of enrollment, the U.S. ranks fifth in the world in the percent of young adults enrolled in college. The leader? Finland. As for those with a four-year college degree, the U.S. ranks twelfth. While 70 percent of high school graduates in the U.S. initially enroll in a bachelor degree program, only slightly more than half receive a degree, according to data from the National Center for Education Statistics. The Center's figures also show that students from the highest income families are almost eight times as likely to earn a bachelors degree as lower-income sons and daughters.

It may surprise some that those who do not attend, nor graduate from college, still represent the vast majority of our population. Data from the National Center for Education Statistics show that, in 2009, among young adults aged twenty-five to twenty-nine,

The Role of Social Safety Nets

only 30 percent had a four-year bachelor's degree; 70 percent did not. A group of this magnitude should certainly not be excluded from opportunities to share in the American Dream. They deserve a pathway to the Dream, equipped with skills that enable them to get good jobs at good wages – not as hamburger-flippers in fast food restaurants, but as workers able to compete with workers in other parts of the world. Vocational schools, or now more commonly known as career and technical schools, have tried to meet this need, but the results have been mediocre here in the U.S. We have a patchwork vocational education system. The nation's 1,200 community colleges try to fill this need. There are also community-funded adult education programs in many cities. And there are the for-profit privately run schools, many of which are now being investigated for deceptive student recruitment practices, exorbitant costs, and over-promises of jobs after one completes their program.

In contrast to the mediocre American system of vocational education, other countries have highly successful youth apprenticeship programs. The German model is one of these, administered by their Federal Ministry of Education. It is a joint undertaking of businesses, government and unions. Today, almost half of young people are participating in German apprenticeship programs that offer training in 350 different occupational categories. Over 500,000 companies are involved with large, small, and medium-size businesses actively participating in the programs. Apprentices work three or four days a week at a company, and are paid by that company at a rate which escalates with each year of training – normally over a three-year period. The German government pays the tuition for the one to two days a week the trainee spends at a vocational school. For the average apprentice, the government funds half the total costs; participating businesses pay the other half.

There are other successful vocational education programs that we can learn from right here closer to home. Our own military services have been leaders in training soldiers, sailors and airmen in the high tech skills now required to maintain a highly professional defense establishment. The Air Force offers perhaps the most extensive programs, administered by its Air Education and Training Command, headquartered outside San Antonio, Texas, at Randolph Air Force Base. Here are some of the key aspects of their programs for newly enlisted personnel.

While completing eight weeks of basic training, new enlistees are given aptitude tests that help guide counselors in the selection of career occupational paths for that individual. There are more than seventy-five such paths, grouped in five technical categories. Most are not only designed to fit the military's needs, but also to have broader civilian applications that can be used if the individual decides to return to civilian life at the expiration of the enlistment period. Such programs include training in aerospace maintenance, electrical systems, heating and air conditioning; medical support services – including biomedical equipment maintenance, diagnostic imaging and surgical assistance services. In electronics, there are twenty-eight different specialties. Classroom instruction is given largely at five different training bases and can range from four to fifty-two weeks in length. The enlistee graduates as an apprentice and is then assigned to a new base for on-the-job training.

In the course of their service commitment, the enlistees can also take advantage of more advanced vocational and academic programs offered by the Community College of the Air Force. With affiliated schools in thirty-seven states and nine overseas locations, two-year accredited Associate's in Applied Sciences degrees are offered in five career areas: Aircraft and Missile Maintenance, Allied Health, Electronics and Telecommunications, Logistics and Resources, and Public and Support Services. The Air Force absorbs the bulk of the costs. By 2010, the program had awarded over 300,000 degrees.

Recently, there has been increased interest in the vocational education models among American educators. In 2008, the Harvard Graduate School of Education initiated a study of vocational training opportunities as part of what it calls, the Pathway to Prosperity Project. Their basic premise is that "college is not for all" and our society's singular focus on those seeking a college education is outdated. The study points out that half of all new jobs in the next decade will go to those with two-year associate's degrees or occupational certificates. In a subsequent report issued in 2011, the study group presented its conclusions in the broader context of our nation's long-term needs:

> The American system for preparing young people to lead productive and prosperous lives as adults is clearly badly broken. Failure to aggressively overcome this challenge will surely erode the fabric of our society. The American Dream rests on the promise of economic opportunity, with a middle-class lifestyle for those willing to work for it. Yet, for the millions of young Americans entering adulthood lacking access to marketable skills, the American Dream may be just an illusion, unlikely ever to come within their grasp.

There is clearly a need that educational opportunities – both college and non-college be addressed by policy makers. In the new era of globalization, where industries and nations must compete with one another, a skilled and educated workforce is essential to national success. The European nations recognize this by publicly supporting higher education – providing it free to their citizens, or at only modest cost. This approach may not totally be the answer to our dilemma, but we have got to find ways to do it.

2. *Good, Stable Jobs at Good Wages*

A second pillar essential to keeping the American Dream alive is that of ensuring good, stable jobs at good wages. In terms of our national interest, the quality of a country's labor force is a key determinant of competitiveness in an era of globalization. Business guru, Peter Drucker, told us, "A country's competitive position in the world economy has to be the first consideration in its domestic policy."

Unfortunately, the new free-market economy has brought with it significant changes in the size, composition, and stability of the nation's workforce. These changes were discussed previously and include the impact of industry deregulation, new technologies and automation, the decline of labor unions, and the effects of globalization on workers. These changes began in the last two decades of the twentieth century, but have really now accelerated.

As pointed out earlier, since the year 2000, there have been two recessions in the U.S. Both have been characterized as "jobless recoveries." Following the 2008-09 recession, and after eighteen months of recovery, the workforce was still 7.5 million jobs below its pre-recession levels. As of mid-year 2010, U.S. employment was just 1.6 percent above where it was at the start of the decade. In contrast, over the same ten-year period, the adult working-age population rose by 12.1 percent.

What has occurred is structural in nature, i.e., not a cyclical situation in which employment traditionally rises to its prior levels following a downturn, but rather what may be new labor market realities: (1) the reluctance of companies to rehire, as they see a long-term slowdown in our country's economic growth, (2) the expanded use of new automated technologies to replace the need for additional workers, (3) offshoring of jobs to low-wage countries. Offshoring is now not only shrinking our domestic blue-collar workforce, but white-collar workers, as well. Princeton professor, Allen Blinder, a highly respected labor economist, did an extensive study of offshoring in which he analyzed 817 different occupations in terms of their vulnerability to offshoring in the years ahead. He found fifty-nine what he termed, "highly offshorable" and another one hundred, fifty-one "offshorable." These vulnerable occupational groups employ thirty-one million workers in the U.S., or approximately 25 percent of our workforce. His net conclusion: one-in-four U.S. workers could find their jobs shipped overseas. These disruptive forces all create job-loss anxiety among the millions of workers potentially impacted by these free-market developments. These factors are not going to go away, but safety nets can work to cushion the blow. Unemployment compensation is one such safety net. Job retraining is another. To

The Role of Social Safety Nets

some extent, these safety nets do exist in the U.S. but could be much improved. Unemployment compensation is paid by the states and normally runs for only twenty-six weeks unless extended with federal funding. In spite of these programs, only half of the unemployed usually qualify for compensation. Job retraining is available in most states but is haphazard and of questionable usefulness in terms of what is provided. Some lessons might be learned from European countries, which provide their workers with much more elaborate safety nets, protecting them in situations where jobs might be or are already lost. Unemployment compensation in most European countries covers workers for a longer time than in the U.S., in some cases for up to three years. Also, the compensation is a lot higher. The German system calculates compensation on the basis of a percentage of net wages, usually up to two-thirds of one's earnings. Most European countries also try to discourage layoffs before they occur. Laws require employers to give between two and six weeks notice to employees they plan to dismiss. In Germany, companies must advise work councils (elected worker representatives) of layoffs planned over the next twelve months. Work-sharing and reduction of hours worked are also encouraged as an alternative to layoffs. Though criticized by many economists as creating inflexible labor markets, these steps do much, not only to lessen the impact of a job loss, but reduce job-security anxieties. In the U.S. the only requirements by law are only for large companies to provide sixty days notice before layoffs of a third or more of employees, or a plant closing.

Work and Family Balance:

The new free-market economy has brought with it significant changes in the characteristics and needs of working households. Today there are almost as many women as men in the labor force. In 60 percent of married couple households, there are two wage earners. Almost two-thirds of women with children are employed. They bring a whole host of new requirements for families – daycare, maternity leave and attention to other personal needs. Most of the industrial nations of the world understand these needs and have addressed them with safety net programs. The United States has not. According to the International Labor Office, more than one hundred, twenty countries mandate *paid* maternity leave, with over half providing fourteen weeks or more. In the U.S., the Family Medical Leave Act of 1993 mandates only twelve weeks of *unpaid* leave, and this is just required in companies with fifty or more employees. Daycare today is another essential for dual-working households. In most European countries, daycare centers are open to all, and publicly funded or available at very low cost. In the U.S., publicly funded centers are only available to the needy. A variety of studies have shown that existing centers in the U.S. are not very well rated by parents using them and that they are expensive. One study shows that the average annual cost for the care of one child is now equivalent to the tuition and fees charged for a year's enrollment at a state university.

Work and Leisure Balance:

It is well known that Americans work harder and longer than workers in any other country. Foreigners see us as a society that "lives to work, rather than works to live." Data from the OECD show the number of weeks worked annually in each of the major industrial countries. The data takes into account the length of the workweek, holiday and vacation time, and absences due to sickness, family leave, and other personal reasons. The data shows 46.2 weeks of work annually in the U.S., 5.5 weeks longer than in the United Kingdom, France, and Germany and 8.5 weeks more than in the Scandinavian countries. In all these countries, and most others in the industrialized world, there are statutory, minimum, annual paid vacations mandated by law. Not so in the United States.

Though the United States is one of the world's leaders in GDP per head (a measure of nations' output of goods and services divided by its population) there is a price we pay for this. If there is a relationship between leisure time and happiness, the absence of this time in the U.S. must certainly inhibit our pursuit of happiness – one of the foundations of the American Dream.

In the new free-market economy in which we live, good, stable jobs at good wages are becoming

115

harder to find. Job stability and security are declining. And new imbalances are emerging in our country between work and family and work and leisure. The European nations are dealing with these issues, creating safety nets and mandates that work for the benefit of their workers. Though these measures may not all be appropriate for the United States, there are some lessons here that one can learn. Unfortunately, our national hubris may be getting in the way and shutting off new ideas from what we consider an old Europe.

3. *Universal Healthcare*

The third area that safety nets can work to sustain the American Dream is healthcare. Individuals with poor health, illnesses, and those who have sustained injury, cannot perform to their full potential and realize the Dream. British statesman and social thinker, Benjamin Disraeli, told us, "The health of the people is really the foundation upon which all their happiness and all their powers as a state depend." Without a healthcare safety net, medical catastrophes can decimate a family's economic well-being, putting them into burdensome debt and shutting off opportunities to enjoy a better life for themselves and their children.

In the U.S., healthcare spending is substantial. In terms of healthcare dollar outlays, we rank first in the world. In spite of this, the ratings given on our healthcare system are extremely low. The World Health Organization ranks us thirty-second in the world, based on its comprehensive rating criteria:

> The extent to which investments in public health and medicine contribute to critical social objectives improving health, reducing health disparities, protecting households from impoverishment due to medical expenses, and providing responsive services that respect the dignity of patients.

The above is a multi-faceted criterion that looks beyond what Americans see as some of the strengths unique to our system – advanced diagnostic techniques, innovations in surgery, breakthroughs in pharmaceutical drugs, and research into new areas of medical science. Yes, we are leaders in these areas, but the best is not good enough if people don't have access to these services, or cannot afford them. As most know, up until now, the U.S. is the only country in the industrial world without a universal healthcare plan that provides open access to medical services for all.

In 2009, the Kaiser Family Foundation reported that, in the U.S., one in five adults under sixty-five were uninsured. This represents 41.7 million individuals, with 8.3 million children uninsured. Their report shows the majority of the uninsured are in working families, but tend to be in low-wage, blue-collar jobs, or to work for small firms. Inequality, which is not supposed to be part of the American Dream, is certainly evident in these healthcare statistics. The U.S. healthcare system, as most know, is tied to one's employment. Government data show 71 percent of employers offering healthcare insurance to their employees on a shared-cost basis. On average, the employer cost contribution is 70 percent; that of the employee is 30 percent. The employee's cost now averages almost $4,000 annually for family coverage. As employers try to contain costs, they have increased the worker's portion much more rapidly than their own share. Additionally, they have raised deductibles. Kaiser data now show 27 percent of workers with annual deductibles of $1,000 or more.

In March of 2010, changes and reform of the U.S. healthcare system were finally put in place as President Obama signed the Patient Protection and Affordable Care Act into law. Most all of its provisions will not become effective until 2014, and they may be modified before then by Congressional action or court rulings. The underlying plan principles will probably remain in place: (1) a plan that is universal in nature covering most all U.S. citizens and legal residents, (2) an employer-based plan rather than a single-payer government plan, and (3) a plan involving the use of private insurance companies. There will be government standards, oversight, and mandates for companies, insurance organizations, and individuals. Direct government

The Role of Social Safety Nets

subsidies will largely be limited to extending Medicaid coverage to a greater number of poorer families.

After years of debate and proposals for universal coverage, the United States will have joined the rest of the industrial world with mandatory universal healthcare coverage, though the U.S. approach to coverage differs from those of other nations. Canada and most of the Scandinavian countries operate single-payer plans that are tax funded, with direct government reimbursement payments made to healthcare providers. Physicians are in private practice. Hospitals are largely non-profit. The United Kingdom has a tax-funded National Health Services (NHS). Physicians are government employees, paid a salary and fees by the NHS. Hospitals are publicly owned as independent trusts. Germany and France operate their plans through Sickness Insurance Funds, which are non-profit government-regulated entities, funded by compulsory employer and employee payroll contributions. Private healthcare providers are paid directly from these funds.

The comparative effectiveness and efficiency of the new U.S. healthcare plan versus those of other nations will have to wait the test of time. What is significant and promising for us is that the anxiety, burdens, and risks of illness or injury will now be protected by a universal safety net – a safety net that will enable Americans to get on with pursuing the Dream. In the words of Scottish essayist Thomas

Carlyle, "He who has health has hope; and he who has hope has everything."

4. *Retirement Security*

Up to now in this chapter, we have discussed what I believe are three of the four basic social needs where safety nets are essential, if we want to restore the American Dream. These are educational opportunities for all, good, stable jobs at good wages, and universal healthcare. The fourth of these is retirement security.

The average American works for more than forty years and looks forward to a comfortable retirement. Just as hard work is essential in realizing the American Dream, so too should there be a reward for this work, with a worry-free retirement. For the nation as a whole, retirement issues today should have a high priority, as an increasing proportion of the population moves into their retirement years. In 2010, there were thirty-nine million Americans aged sixty-five and over. The next decade is going to see this group mushroom in size to fifty-three million, a 35-percent increase in a period when all other age groups will increase by just 4 percent. These new senior citizens are the so-called "baby boomers," seventy-six million strong, born between the years 1946 and 1964. The first of these turns sixty-five in 2011.

Many Americans do retire comfortably. A great many others do not. On an overall basis there is

The Role of Social Safety Nets

a significant gap between the funds we have accumulated for retirement and what we should have to maintain our current standard of living. The Center for Retirement Research at Boston College calculates that, on a national basis, this deficiency is a staggering $6 trillion.

In comparison to other industrialized nations, our retirement system does not rate very well. Each year, a worldwide pension system ranking is published as the Melbourne Mercer Global Pension Index. It shows ratings and rankings for fourteen major industrial nations. In the most recent study, the U.S. ranked tenth, given a letter grade of "C." As in other quality-of-life measures, European countries ranked highest.

Most readers are familiar with what makes up the American retirement system. It is a patchwork mix, comprised of the government Social Security program, public and private sector employer retirement plans, and individual retirement and savings plans. Social Security is the only truly universal plan, and the foundation on which most Americans build their retirement programs. Enacted in 1935, in 2010 government figures show the average payment to recipients of $13,835 annually and for the average married couple, $22,512. Studies show Social Security covering an average of 41 percent of an individual's pre-retirement income, compared to the 70 percent or more experts say is necessary for one to maintain pre-retirement standards of living.

Public and private sector employer plans take a variety of forms. Defined benefit plans, at one time the most extensive of plans among large and medium-size companies, are now quite limited. In these plans, the employer alone sets aside funds, manages the plan, and upon retirement pays the employee a fixed monthly benefit based on formulas typically involving age, salary and length of service. It is guaranteed and paid for life, similar to an annuity. In the 1980s, almost two-thirds of major private-sector employers had such plans. Today it is down to less than 20 percent in the private sector. Only public workers benefit today from these plans that cover 80 percent of their workers. The defined benefit plans were another victim of the free-market economy, as companies saw the need to reduce their employee cost burdens. These earlier plans usually cost them the equivalent of 8 percent of wages paid. Other low-cost alternatives could be found.

Defined contribution plans, largely 401(k)s, have been that alternative, costing companies only an average of 3 percent of worker wages. Employers typically match an employee's contribution to the plans, up to a certain percentage limit and wage level. Workers are given a range of investment options. The plans are portable, so that, if the employee leaves the company, the funds can be withdrawn and "rolled-over" into a tax deferred Individual Retirement Account (IRA), held in the individual's name. Separately, individuals can set aside additional portions of their own wages in these tax-free IRAs, with maximums specified by the government. For self-employed persons, Keogh plans are based on the same principle, i.e., individual, tax-deferred savings set aside by the business owner.

The movement away from defined benefit to 401(k) plans is another example of businesses shifting a large portion of retirement responsibility and risks onto the backs of the workers. Defined benefit plans guaranteed income for life, and they were federally insured in the event of a company's default. With a 401(k) or IRA, the employees are on their own. When the stock market plummeted in the 2008-09 recession, their retirement accounts also tumbled. Investment Company Institute data show half of 401(k) and IRA accounts are in mutual funds, and two-thirds of these in the more volatile stock equity funds. Both carry risks and no guarantees.

Coverage and the payment benefits provided by the 401(k) plans are also not what most realize. A variety of independent research organizations report that just over half of U.S. employees work for companies who sponsor such plans. And in these companies, more than one-in-five of the employees choose not to participate in the plans at all. Of those who do participate, nearly half do not contribute enough to match their company's contribution. Further depressing the amounts saved in the plans are employee loan withdrawals in hardship situations and "cash-outs," i.e., failing to roll over the funds into an IRA account when leaving the company. When all these factors are considered, the net effect is that a substantial portion of workers really have-less-than adequate pension coverage or savings. Federal Reserve Board figures show that for married couple households headed by individuals now between forty-five and fifty-four, median retirement assets (excepting Social Security entitlement) were $103,200 in 2010 dollars. Assuming fifteen years in retirement with the funds returning 6 percent annually, and an inflation rate of 2 percent, the payout from these savings would be just $765 a month.

Surveys among Americans relating to their confidence in having enough saved for retirement all show extremely low levels of optimism. Annual studies by the Employee Benefit Research Institute show those feeling "very confident" about their retirement income situation hovering only in the 20-percent range. The problem is particularly acute for low-earning households whose participation and contribution to pension plans have been limited. For these households, one study shows 70 percent of low-wage earners will be dependent almost entirely on Social Security. Unlike in Europe, where worker retirement payouts are universal and proportionate to income, inequality is built into the American system. In Europe, the average retiree's pension covers 70 percent of pre-retirement savings – a percentage noted earlier that most experts say is needed to match pre-retirement standards of living. The U.S. is obviously well below this norm.

In this chapter, we have suggested that an important step toward restoring the American Dream is to consider what social safety nets can do. We pointed out that safety nets can work to cushion the blow of the changes and turbulence, which the new free-market economy has wrought. The European experience with these safety nets has been extensive, and there are lessons here that can be helpful in shaping social policies in our country.

There are four areas of need that are essential if we want to restore the American Dream. These are areas that are an integral part of the Dream – educational opportunities for all, good stable jobs at good wages, universal healthcare, and a secure retirement.

CHAPTER 7

Restoration Agenda and Responsibilities

"We are made wise not to be recollections of our past, but by the responsibility for our future."

-George Bernard Shaw

In this final chapter we look at how the American Dream can be restored – a dream of equal opportunity for all, upward mobility, and a better life for our children. What is not here in this last chapter is a list of specific programs or policy recommendations that are usually included in books of this kind, written by scholars or social policy experts. I am neither of these. I do however, have four decades of experience in problem solving in the business world. Over these years, I learned that the process starts with correctly defining the problem – its severity, scope and complexity. Next comes a thorough analysis of that problem – its causes and extent of its impact on stakeholders. I think we have done these in the first sections of this book in an objective manner with factual data. As the late U.S. senator Daniel P. Moynihan said, "Everyone is entitled to their own opinions, but not their own facts." I have tried my best to be factual.

With the problem of the Dream's erosion identified and analyzed, one can then move on to outlining a restoration agenda and defining where the responsibilities should lie for restoring the Dream. Let's begin with an agenda, and then move on to responsibilities.

Step #1
Understand the realities – both positive and negative – of the new global, free-market economic environment in which we now live.

It will surprise many that important business leaders, economists, government officials, and segments of the public still fight the free-market realities that are at work today, or are in denial about their existence. Many unions and free-trade proponents still want protectionist tariffs. Many economists believe that the Great Recession of 2008-09 was just a short-term cyclical downturn and did not represent a longer-term structural change in a free-market economy. Let's get with it. The free-market economy is here to stay – globalization, new technologies and automation, deregulation, and privatization. Much good has and will come from these changes, but there are also the disruptive factors that accompany a transition between an old and new economy. Historically, this happened in our nation with a change from an agricultural economy to an industrial one, and then from an industrial one to a service and information economy. Only with a recognition that the free-market is here to stay, will we be able to deal with issues related to it. As lyricist Johnny Mercer once wrote, we have got to find a way to "accentuate the positives and eliminate the negatives." Let's find a way to do both.

Step #2
Redefine the kind of society we want to be and, where necessary, reorder our national priorities.

The U.S. Constitution, adopted in 1787, along with its later Amendments, defined what we would stand for as a nation. Over time, political leaders, social activists and others have also presented us with their vision of what America should be in terms of its core values and ideology. Though these represent goals and aspirations, what we are is shaped by what we do – the legislation that is enacted, court rulings, and how we spend our tax revenues and the priorities that they reflect. The largest category of spending in the federal budget today is outlays for the Department of Defense. Now, approximately $700 billion in 2011 we spend more on defense than the rest of the world combined. And, realistically, these outlays

The American Dream

are not just to defend our nation, but also to finance intervention and preemptive military strikes where we see them to be in America's best interest. In 1949, the Defense Department took on its current name, changing from what was then called the War Department. Perhaps that should now be reversed.

In a thought-provoking book by Andrew J Bacevil, *Washington Rules: America's Path to Permanent War,* this retired military officer sets forth the premise that our nation's credo is now almost totally defined by our goals "to lead, save, and ultimately transform the world." He points out that from the end of World War II to the present, regardless of the administration in power, this ethos has become more and more embedded in our culture. He points out there are now 760 U.S. military bases in thirty-nine different countries, with 300,000 troops deployed and another 90,000 at sea in six navy carrier strike groups. We divide the world into so-called "commands," each with its own elaborate military structure. In January of 1961, in his farewell address to the nation, President Eisenhower warned us of the danger inherent in the growth of a military-industrial complex, a marriage of a nation's military and industrial policy.

> "In the councils of government, we must guard against the acquisition of unwarranted influence, whether sought or unsought, by the military-industrial complex. The potential for the disastrous rise of misplaced power

exists and will persist. We must never let the weight of this combination endanger our liberties of democratic process."

As a nation, we have paid little attention to his warning. Since 2000, defense spending has increased at an annual rate of 9 percent, and this excludes the costs of the wars in Iraq and Afghanistan. What is significant is that expenditures of this magnitude limit what is available to spend on domestic safety net programs that could help us restore the American Dream. The nation's priorities certainly need to be reexamined. Do we really want to save the world, or our own nation?

Step #3
Create a better balance between economic and non-economic quality-of-life aspiration for our citizens.

Many people in other parts of the world see America as a materialistic country. Though the American Dream has important economic factors built within it, the Dream is much more than that, starting with the Declaration of Independence, which spoke of "life, liberty, and the pursuit of happiness."

Many social scientists today question how we measure our success as a nation. Unfortunately, we do it largely with economic measures, gross domestic product, industrial production output, national income, etc. Why, they say, can't we do the same for non-economic quality-of-life measurements? We noted in an earlier chapter that such organization as the United Nations have developed such measures, and periodically rank their member nations. One metric is the United Nations Human Development Index, a composite index measuring the health, knowledge, and standards of living of a given country. In 2000, the U.S. ranked just thirteenth, well behind Canada, four Scandinavian countries, and eight others in different parts of the world. In contrast to this low U.S. quality-of-life rating, our country usually ranks at the top on economic measurements.

In the forefront of countries that are attempting to gain greater insight into the quality-of-life of their citizens is the Canadian government. In 2009, it announced plans for issuance of a new set of measures on quality-of-life. Called the Canadian Index of Well-Being (CIW), the government pointed out, "Most Canadians realize that their well-being is not measured by just narrow measures like GDP." The new CIW index will, on a continuing basis, measure the things that matter most to Canadians."

The new Canadian measures will report on eight aspects of life: standards of living, health, community vitality, education, leisure time, participation in the democratic process, arts/culture/recreation, and environmental quality. Full reports and composite statistical measures will be published for each of these areas. Where relevant, the reports will also combine economic measures with non-economic ones. For example, the report on standards of living will include nine areas of analysis:

- After-tax Median Income
- Income Distribution
- Incidence of Low Income
- Wealth Distribution
- Economic Security
- Long-term Unemployment
- Employment Rate
- Employment Quality
- Housing Standards and Affordability

Quite an undertaking, and perhaps a model for our own American Dream index.

Step #4
We should not be reluctant to learn from the experience of other nations with the use of social safety nets.

In Chapter 6, we spent a good deal of time examining the different kinds of social safety nets used by European countries to minimize risks and economic shocks that impact their citizens. We did this because there can be lessons to be learned. It is true that today the European countries are questioning whether they can financially sustain such programs, and many may therefore have to be cut back, or some might have to be discarded completely. Regardless of their long-term viability, we can still learn a lot from the more than fifty years of experience European nations have had using a variety of social safety net programs.

American hubris, and an attitude in some sectors of the population that "America knows best" have got in the way of these learning opportunities. When was the last time we heard about a congressional delegation or study group going to Europe to review the world-renowned Scandinavian social safety net systems. Unfortunately, many leading government officials mock the social capitalism ideas of these countries. They are just "old Europe," and "we know best."

If we were to swallow our pride and attitudes of exceptionalism, we would study the European programs, not from the standpoint of whether to change our way of life and adopt theirs, but rather to learn what new ideas we can extract from the individual parts of their systems – in employment practices, education, healthcare, and retirement security. Here are some examples of specific areas of investigation that might be undertaken. Some have been discussed earlier.

A variety of studies now show that our country's ranking in educational achievement is sliding badly. In order to compete in a new global environment, we have noted earlier that an educated workforce is an essential. Otherwise, we will see our standards of living slide, income inequality rise, and opportunities for achieving the American Dream erode. In contrast to the low ratings we are seeing, the educational achievement ratings for other nations are increasing. In 2010, a UNICEF study titled, "The Children Left Behind," showed a U.S. worldwide education ranking of thirteenth in math and twenty-fourth in science literacy. Which nation held the top rating? Finland, in both math and science. Wouldn't it be wise for us to investigate why there is such a divergence between our ratings and theirs? I am sure the Finish National Board of Education would welcome an American delegation that wanted to examine its systems and its obvious strengths.

A second learning opportunity relates to employment of our young people – those beginning their search for achieving the American Dream. If today's statistics hold, 70 percent of our youth will not earn a four-year college degree, but will still be looking for good jobs at good wages. In an earlier chapter, we pointed out that the German government recognizes this in its own data and understands the importance of non-college young people. They also know that vocational training and skills are necessary if these individuals are to get those good jobs at good wages and make the German workforce competitive in the world's labor markets. The means to that end is their highly successful apprenticeship programs, which were discussed in the last chapter. Again, wouldn't it be wise for us to study the strengths of their program?

A third example of what and where we might borrow on the experience of other nations is in policies relating to working families. The International Labor Organization (ILO) tells us that, in the industrialized nations of the world, almost 80 percent of women work outside the home in their child-bearing years. In one-hundred, twenty countries, *paid* maternity leave and benefits are mandated by law. In the U.S., it is *unpaid* leave at just twelve weeks. As in most social legislation, the Scandinavian countries have been leaders in helping their citizens' better balance work and family life. Norway would be a good model for study. It even extends mandated family leave policies to include fathers.

In helping repair the American Dream, these are but a few examples of where bits and pieces of social safety nets might be extracted without wholesale adoption of the entire safety net. At least they are worth examining.

Step #5
Create a new three-way partnership among government, businesses, and the public to work out the steps necessary to restore the American Dream.

Some readers may have concluded that I would take a socialistic approach to rebuilding the American Dream. That I believe we should adopt the European social capitalist systems, and that it is government's responsibility to put programs in place that will restore the Dream. This is not the case, for a number of reasons. Government can do some things to address the issues involved in restoring the Dream. It can lead, encourage and provide incentives, but it will have difficulty if it tries to mandate. That is evident now in court challenges to the newly-enacted healthcare legislation. It is evident in the Republican Party's strong resistance to social legislation, now with a majority position in the House of Representatives. It is evident in the rise of the Tea Party and its demand for smaller government.

Businesses are also hamstrung in many ways in repairing the Dream. Globalization has heightened competition, forcing businesses to drive down their costs. As we have shown earlier, that is why companies have cut employee benefits, shifting responsibilities back to their workers. Corporate lobbyists will continue to have a strong voice in Washington, and will oppose any government actions that would increase business operating costs.

And there is the general public, vulnerable to outside economic turbulence and in some respects powerless. This is not to say the public is made up of victims. They too have walked away from the Dream, by years of excess, self-indulgence, overspending and borrowing – behavior patterns that the thrifty Puritans would have abhorred.

If no one of the three parties can restore the Dream alone, there has to be a joint effort, shared responsibility, a give-and-take, and a willingness to compromise one's own self-interests. The partnership also must be one that is organized and structured with joint study groups. There might be an overseer coordinating an American Dream study group, but also sub-groups whose focus is on what we have defined as the four pillars of the Dream – education, employment, healthcare and retirement security. Representing the government would be congressional leaders. Businesses would be represented by CEOs of major companies and trade association heads. The public's representatives would be union leaders and officials from various consumer advocate groups. Each of the study groups – the overseer group and the sub-groups would have membership comprised of government, businesses and citizen representatives.

Partner Responsibilities

Let's now examine what each of the three partners should bring to the table.

Government Responsibilities

The starting point, and most significant contribution of government, is to do what has been outlined earlier – define the kind of society we want to be. Is it a society that is built on its economic pre-eminence? Its military power? Or its values? If the latter, what are these values? Highly-respected *New York Times* columnist David Brooks provided insight into these questions in a November 2010 column:

> "Since World War II, we have built our national identity on our rank among nations...the U.S. will have to learn to define itself not by

rank, but by its values. It will be important to have the right story to tell, the right purpose, and the right aura. It will be more important to know who we are."

Government's role in helping restore the Dream is to take the lead, using the bully pulpit, with congressional leaders, cabinet members, and those in the executive branch redefining and communicating to the public what we stand for. Government can also challenge its other two partners to join with it, suggesting cooperative actions that businesses and the public can take that will help restore the Dream.

Congressional gridlock perhaps will end if the two political parties see a common and worthwhile goal that has to be met. They have also got to take a macro point of view in tackling the issues that have to be dealt with – built around the four pillars of the Dream that we have identified. Too much of our Washington focus is on only small pieces of the broader issues, resulting in patchwork solutions to our national problems. For example, school vouchers or Pell Grants are micro issues. Education opportunities are the macro issue. Similarly, Medicare should also not be examined by itself. Healthcare for all is the issue. The same holds true for Social Security. Yes, it is important, but the broader issue is retirement security for all Americans. Unlike European governments that have defined policies around macro issues, in the U.S., we always seem to deal with just pieces of the larger whole that satisfy the needs of a few self-interest groups.

Business Responsibilities

Earlier in the book, we pointed out how businesses, perhaps unknowingly, contributed to the erosion of the Dream, largely by shifting risks present in the free-market economy onto the backs of their employees. Job security diminished, employee benefits such as pensions were cut back drastically. Wall Street became their primary focus, reflected in business models that redefined a company's goals as one primarily to build shareholder value. So-called stakeholders became of secondary concern – employees, customers, suppliers, the community and the environment. Emerging lately is the interest well-known business scholars, consultants, and innovative companies are giving to the concept of *shared value.* Harvard University professors Michael E. Porter and Mark P. Kramer, in a widely read *Harvard Business Review* article, state:

> Shared value involves creating economic value in a way that also creates value for society by addressing its needs and challenges. Shared value is not social responsibility or philanthropy, but a new way to achieve economic success.

Restoration Agenda and Responsibilities

A starting point for business leaders is to rethink their operating practices with this kind of fresh thinking – understanding that they have been self-serving and their values no longer fit into the kind of society envisioned in the American Dream. A second responsibility of businesses, if they want to participate in the restoration of the Dream, is to give their employees a more equal share of the rewards that come with increased corporate profitability. Though employees have become more and more productive, they have seen few rewards from this increased productivity. Two years after recovery from the 2008-09 recession, corporate profits reached historic highs. Corporations were sitting on trillions of dollars in cash. Though employee productivity has increased by 29 percent since the year 2000, average hourly earnings, on an inflation-adjusted basis, for production and non-supervisory workers are up by a meager 7 percent, less than a quarter of the productivity gain.

If businesses were to begin to share their income more fairly with their average worker, higher wages and salaries would help reinvigorate middle-class economic well-being and arrest the trend toward income inequality that works to erode the Dream. Workers could also use a portion of these give-backs to restore many of the company benefits they once enjoyed. One of these is retirement. We all recognize that companies are never going to restore the defined benefit pension plans that existed in early post-war America. The 401(k) is now its replacement. Companies set the amount of their maximum annual contributions in percentage terms, and with an earnings ceiling. Also set is the employee's maximum contribution. Employer contributions to these plans could be increased and accompanied by changes in the employee's contributions. These increases could go a long way toward giving Americans the kind of retirement income needed to supplement what they receive in Social Security benefits.

Another way businesses can help restore the Dream for younger workers is with a consideration of apprenticeship programs that we have discussed earlier. From an overall conceptual point of view, businesses can and should play an active role in restoring the Dream – not as a result of government mandates, but with recognition on their own that it is a national economic necessity. Economist and former Labor Secretary Robert Reich has said that, "until and unless America's vast middle and working classes gain a larger share of the gains of economic growth, our country will never fully recover from its doldrums." He was referring to the long and protracted 2010-11 economic recovery. From a self-interest standpoint, businesses should also understand that the hollowing-out of the middle class that is now occurring is destroying their own customer base. Who is going to buy their cars and household appliances? Henry Ford commented many years ago when he gave his employees a $5.00 daily wage: "I want them to be able to afford to buy my cars."

The above initiatives by businesses should be structured to strengthen our domestic market and American workers. Unfortunately, the focus of many multi-national American companies today is on international markets. General Motors now sells more cars in China each year than in the United States. Among S & P 500 companies, 48 percent of revenues are now generated from international operations. Though overseas opportunities are enticing for these companies, they do have a responsibility to our citizens in our country.

Individual Responsibilities

The American Dream is a dream of individuals, and these individuals have to bear some of the responsibility for its erosion. They were not innocent bystanders to what has occurred over the past thirty years. They violated most all of the principles set forth by those who created and enhanced the Dream – the thrift lessons of the Puritans and Ben Franklin, the immigrants who saved to send their children to college.

What we have seen over the last three decades is Americans living beyond their means. It shows in a whole host of measures – historic lows in savings rates, historic highs in household debt. American homes became, not part of the Dream envisioned by the homesteader, but rather a piggy bank from which money could be withdrawn through mortgage refinancing and home equity loans. One's home became a speculative asset. The credit card became the means through which needs could be satisfied today, rather than by waiting and saving for the purchase tomorrow.

This overspending increased the vulnerability of the average household to economic shocks. And one of these occurred in 2008-09. Households are now deleveraging. Attitude studies show that households may have learned their lessons and are now embracing a "new normal," characterized by thrift, reduction in unnecessary spending, higher savings and avoidance of new debt obligations. Time will tell us whether these are in fact a "new normal," or whether Americans will revert to their old ways. If they do go backwards, they will destroy any chances of restoring the Dream.

Individuals have another challenge. If they want their government and business partners to work with them in restoring the Dream, they have got to become more active participants in our democracy by not electing government representatives and others opposed to their self-interests. The level of active participation in our democracy can be summed up in one single statistic: the percent of eligible voters who cast a ballot in national elections. In 2008, with the election of Barack Obama - though a recent high - it was just 57.4 percent. Historically, the peak was only with the election of John F. Kennedy in 1960, when the turnout was 63.1 percent.

Further compounding the low voter turnout is that many who do vote have a low awareness of key issues and vote on the basis of personalities or negative perceptions of a candidate (voting against someone, not for someone). Another factor is the degree to which a party or its candidates exploit emotional/cultural issues that have little bearing on the public's real needs. Following the 2004 national election, author Robert Frank wrote an insightful analysis of this phenomenon in his book, *What's the Matter with Kansas*. He notes that millions of voters cast their ballots for those "less likely to protect their safety, less likely to protect their jobs, and less likely to benefit them economically." They were divided, he says by emotional cultural issues such as abortion, gun control, bible reading, and flag burning – none of which will ever be dealt with after their candidate is elected.

Individuals can, through their own changes in behavior, help restore the Dream. They can also become much active participants in their democracy and influence government, which in turn, can gain the support of the business community.

The steps necessary to restore the Dream will not be easy ones. They begin with understanding that the free-market economic changes are significant ones, and we therefore may have to redefine the kind of society we want to be and what the balance should be between our economic and non-economic values. As we deal with these issues, we can learn from the experience of other nations, even though many of them have taken different approaches to social policy than we have – through the use of elaborate social safety nets. In reality, that is not going to happen here, and it therefore is necessary for us to address our problems through a new kind of three-way partnership among government, businesses and individuals. There will have to be a give-and-take among the partners, but working together, we can restore the Dream.

CONCLUSION

One of the most difficult things for any of us to do is to recognize, understand and accept changes that are occurring in the world around us. Change is uncomfortable; the status quo is much more comfortable. Change can be subtle or complex, with multiple dimensions that are difficult to unravel. Change represents uncertainty. And, when change occurs, many of us still remain in a state of denial. It is not happening, or it does not affect me. All these are psychological barriers that have to be overcome. As the late John F. Kennedy said, "Change is the law of life and those who only look to the past or present are certain to miss the future."

The premise set forth in this book is that fundamental changes in our nation's economy have now occurred, and let us therefore accept them. The new free-market economy has brought with it disruptive forces that have to be dealt with by our government, businesses and everyday citizens. They are not short-term cyclical problems that will go away. Nevertheless, we seem to be in a state of economic myopia. The word *myopia* is of Greek origin. Normally it deals with an eye impairment, meaning optical vision that is nearsighted. To be myopic is to be able to see clearly up close, but almost everything else in the distance is blurred. In the context of this book, it follows that *economic myopia* means that though we may now be experiencing and understand the short-term effects of the new free-market economy, we do not see or want to see the real and more significant longer-term implications.

I believe the evidence that change is upon us is irrefutable. All we have to do is connect the dots, to borrow a phrase commonly used by trend analysis. It calls for connecting what appear to be single, unrelated situations with others, to see if there is a common thread. Analysts in the nation's intelligence services require that conclusions never be drawn from a single piece of intelligence. Their challenge is to find other related pieces of evidence and then "connect the dots." Most failures in intelligence result not, from flawed single findings, but rather in an inability on the part of analysts to connect one piece of intelligence to another.

In Chapter 4, we identified eight factors that support our premise that the American Dream is eroding. These were dots that we connected to draw this conclusion:

- Industry deregulation
- Decline of labor unions

- New technologies & automation
- New economy business cycles

- Globalization
- Income stagnation and inequality

- Changes in business management practices

- Consumer excess

CONCLUSION

If, as a reader, you come to the same conclusions and accept the fact that changes have occurred in our economy that threaten the survival of the Dream, then it is only logical that we act to remedy the situation.

In a broader sense, what is evident is that unfettered free-market capitalism, in its present form, does not work for the benefit of the broad base of American households. In a worldwide survey of attitudes toward capitalism, conducted in 2010 by Globe Scan, an international public opinion research firm, only 59 percent of Americans felt that "the free-market economy is the best economic system." This is down from 80 percent in a comparable 2002 survey, and 64 percent in 2009. Should we therefore abandon capitalism? No. Capitalism can be made to work for our benefit, if we just build in protective safeguards that do two important things: (1) preserve *upside* opportunities for all of us, and (2) minimize unforeseen and potentially catastrophic *downside* risks to our economic well-being. Both of these goals can be accomplished selectively using some of the social safety nets discussed in earlier chapters. These safety nets do not have to be in the form of government handouts or so-called entitlements. There is growing concern that such programs will enlarge the worsening national deficit, and must therefore be cut back, rather than expanded – Medicare, Medicaid, and Social Security, to name a few of the programs now being scrutinized. Unfortunately, we are reluctant to consider higher taxes as an alternative way of sustaining these and other new programs. For Americans, such taxes cannot be looked at as an added burden. Rather, they should be viewed the same way as insurance purchases are. They are outlays that buy protection against risk and uncertainty. Higher taxes, yes, but more protection against the downside risks now inherent in a free-market economy.

Acting collectively, government, businesses, and we as individuals, should take a vow that we are going to act now to restore and preserve the American Dream for our children and grandchildren. This vow is presented on the final page of our book. It is in the form of a Peoples' Proclamation.

* * *

CONCLUSION

THE AMERICAN DREAM

We the people of the United States are a nation founded and built on a unique set of ideals and values. Ours is a nation where equality exists for everyone. Regardless of gender, race, or ethnic origin, each of us has the same opportunities as others to achieve high standards of living and a better quality of life.

We recognize that to fulfill these aspirations we must have an educated citizenry, with a strong work ethic. And we must be frugal and not self-indulgent in our everyday living. Individualism is one of our core values, and we must therefore be resourceful and self-reliant. We are a self-confident, optimistic, and forward-looking people, with high expectations for ourselves and our children.

We want our offspring to have even fuller and richer lives than ours. We have lived by the words set forth in our Declaration of Independence: that we have certain unalienable rights – life, liberty, and the pursuit of happiness. The American Dream represents the cultural values that have guided us in exercising these rights and building a nation that commands the admiration of peoples around the world. Because the Dream has contributed so much to our well-being and the nation's preeminence, we resolve that we will not let it erode, and will work to preserve it for future generations of Americans.

We believe that the preservation of the Dream will require forging a three-way partnership between government, business, and ourselves. Acting together, and where necessary, we may have to make use of social safety nets to guarantee upward opportunities for all our citizens, and at the same time minimize the downward risks our people face in the new free-market economy in which we live.

AUTHOR POSTCRIPT

Readers will recall that in Chapter 2 there was an extended discussion of the role immigrants played in building the American Dream. Immigrant success stories were cited, particularly those of familiar notables. But there are other stories that may not be recognizable at all – personal ones, important to many of us who are the sons and daughters of immigrants. One of these stories follows.

In May of 1906, an Italian steamship entered New York Harbor, passed the Statue of Liberty and then debarked its passengers on Ellis Island, where, before its closing in 1954, twelve million immigrants were processed. Aboard was a five-year-old boy named Vincenzo. He was traveling with an aunt. Both had lived in a small mountain town in southern Italy, then boarded their ship in Naples, and were headed to America as immigrants. They went through immigration screening at Ellis Island and proceeded to Revere, Massachusetts, just outside of Boston, where they would live with relatives who had arrived a few years earlier.

Young Vincenzo, speaking no English, was enrolled in grammar school. He quickly learned what would be his new language and excelled, graduating high school at near the top of his class. His high school performance earned him a full scholarship to Tufts University, a leading New England private institution, and one close enough for him to commute daily from home to his classes. While in college he became a naturalized U.S. citizen, and at the same time took on a new Americanized first name – James. At Tufts, he majored in biology, and with honors grades had hopes of someday becoming a doctor. This dream would soon be realized. He had quickly learned that anything in America is possible. He was accepted at Harvard Medical School, again with a scholarship, and graduated with an M.D. degree in 1929.

Rather than internship in a private hospital, the young doctor chose to do it in the U.S. Navy, which offered medical school graduates a commission with good pay and benefits. He enjoyed his life as a naval officer. Though he considered leaving military service after a few years and going into private practice, the 1930s Depression era was not necessarily a good time to venture out on one's own. At the end of the decade, the Depression would end, but then came World War II, and there would be no military discharges for anyone. At the outbreak of the war, this naval medical officer was 40 years old. He would now be away from his wife and three children for most all of the war, serving on ships in the North Atlantic until he was sent to the Pacific theater. There, assigned to the Second Marine Division, he

AUTHOR POSTCRIPT

went ashore at Okinawa shortly after the April 1945 assault landing and served as head of a field medical hospital until the war ended. He retired as a Commander in 1947 after eighteen years of service.

After the war, in private medical practice, he was a highly-respected ophthalmologist. During those postwar years he was always proud of his military service. He wore a Bronze Star button on his suit lapel. He had been awarded the medal for his meritorious service during the Okinawa campaign. He died in 1980, and as he had requested, was buried in his naval officer's uniform. As is traditional at graveside, the flag was draped over his casket, then smartly folded and presented to his widow. He had lived the American Dream, but always felt he had to give something back to a country that did so much for him. It was a true immigrant's story.

Commander James J. Cammisa, M.D., United States Navy Retired, was this individual, and my father, to whose memory this book is dedicated.

One of the reasons this story has been included here is that readers may have similar ones about their own parents or grandparents who have lived the American Dream. If so, try to reconstruct and preserve their stories – perhaps with an audio or video recording, a photo album, or scrapbook. Highlight the aspects of the Dream that we have discussed in this book that were personally experienced by them. The materials will be a priceless family legacy. Good luck.

J.V.C.

APPENDIX

A - Historic Milestones

B - Economic Well-Being

C - Quality of Life

D - Social Safety Nets

APPENDIX A

Historic Milestones

A – 1 Historic Federal Actions

A – 2 Equality – U.S. Constitutional Amendments

A – 3 Territorial Expansion – Continental U.S.

A – 4 Upward Mobility – Historic Legislative Milestones

The American Dream

A – 1

HISTORIC FEDERAL ACTIONS

Declaration of Independence – 1776

Preamble to the Declaration states that "we hold these Truths to be self-evident that all men are created equal" . . . . .

U.S. Constitution – 1787

Preamble states that "We the People" are the government with the Constitution defining the powers and limitations of government.

Emancipation Proclamation – 1863

An executive order by President Lincoln proclaiming freedom for the nation's slave population. Followed by 14th Amendment to the Constitution.

Brown vs. Board of Education of Topeka – 1954

Supreme Court ruling declared state laws that called for separate public schools of black and white students unconstitutional.

Civil Rights Act of 1964

Outlawed major forms of racial and gender discrimination in voter registration, segregation in schools, workplace and public facilities.

APPENDIX A

Voting Rights Act of 1965

Outlawed discriminatory voting practices and qualification requirements that denied rights of citizens to vote regardless of race or color.

Americans with Disabilities Act of 1990

Prohibited discrimination to Americans with disabilities in employment, use of public transportaion facilities and accommodations.

EQUALITY – U.S. CONSTITUTIONAL AMENDMENTS

Amendment	Text Excerpt	Enactment Date
XIII	Neither slavery nor involuntary servitude shall exist within the United States or any place subject to their jurisdiction.	December 1865
XIV	No state shall make or enforce any law which shall abridge the privileges or immunities of citizens of the United States; nor shall any State deprive any person of life, liberty, or property, without due process of law; nor deny to any person within its jurisdiction the equal protection of the laws.	July 1868

XV	The right of citizens of the United States to vote shall not be denied or abridged by the United States or by any State on account of race, color, or previous condition of servitude.	February 1870
XIX	The rights of citizens of the United States shall not be denied or abridged by the United States or by any State on account of sex.	August 1920

A-3

TERRITORIAL EXPANSION
CONTINENTAL UNITED STATES

	Acquisition	Area	How Acquired
Phase #1 1803	Louisiana Purchase	Mississippi River to Rocky Mountains	Purchased from France
Phase #2 1819	Florida	Florida	Treaty with Spain
Phase #3 1845	Texas	Texas	Annexation
1846	Oregon Country	Washington/Oregon	Treaty with Britain
1848	Mexico Cessation*	California & Southwest	Conquest

Gadsen Purchase was made from Mexico in 1853 adding Southern Arizona and Southwest New Mexico areas.

UPWARD MOBILITY
HISTORIC LEGISLATIVE MILESTONES

Homestead Act of 1862

Granted adult heads of household 160 acres of surveyed public land for a minimum filing fee and promise of 5 years of continued residence.

Morill Act of 1862

Grants of federal land to the States for establishment of land grant colleges.

National Labor Relations Act of 1935

Defined and prohibited unfair company labor practices protecting workers' right to organize and negotiate terms and conditions of employment.

Serviceman's Readjustment Act of 1944

Known as the GI Bill, it provided returning WWII veterans with unemployment compensation, home and business loans, and payments for college and vocational training.

APPENDIX B

Economic Well-Being

B-1 Economic Performance Measures - Worldwide Rankings

B-2 Comparative National Military Expenditures

B-3 Trends in Median Household Income

B-4 Median Family Income by Presence of Wife in Labor Force

B-5 Median Household Income by Level of Educational Attainment

B-6 Trends in Concentrations of Income by Quintile Group

B-7 Trends in Share of Aggregate Income – Top 5% of Households

B-8 Comparative Ratios of Highest vs. Lowest Median Income

B-9 Country Income Inequality – Gini Index

B-10 Employee Compensation vs. Productivity Gains

B-11 Decline in U.S. Manufacturing Employment

ECONOMIC PERFORMANCE MEASURES WORLDWIDE RANKINGS

	U.S.	Canada	United Kingdom	Germany	Japan
Business Environment	6	3	10	13	28
Global Competitiveness	1	10	20	16	24
Innovation	1	12	18	11	3
Information/ Communication/ Technology	5	17	15	21	19
R&D Spending % GDP	6	15	16	10	4
Patents Per M Population	15	18	9	16	6

Source: The Economist Intelligence Unit, 2006

COMPARATIVE NATIONAL MILITARY EXPENDITURES
(Billions of Dollars)

United States	$661.0
China	$102.0
France	$63.9
United Kingdom	$58.3
Russia (est.)	$53.3
Japan	$51.0
Germany	$45.6
Saudi Arabia	$41.2

Source: Stockholm International Peace Research Institute, 2009

TRENDS IN MEDIAN
U.S. HOUSEHOLD INCOME

		Percent Period Change
1980	$ 43,892	-%
1985	$ 44,898	2.3
1990	$ 47,637	6.1
1995	$ 47,622	(0.1)
2000	$ 52,301	9.8
2009	$ 49,777	(4.8)

Source: U.S. Census Bureau, Data in 2009 dollars

MEDIAN FAMILY INCOME BY PRESENCE OF WIFE IN LABOR FORCE

	Not in Labor Force	In Labor Force
1979	$ 47,128	$ 66,173
1989	$ 46,413	$ 73,083
2000	$ 48,140	$ 83,361
2007	$ 47,329	$ 86,435

Source: U.S. Census Bureau/Economic Policy Institute, 2007 dollars

MEDIAN U.S. HOUSEHOLD INCOME BY LEVEL OF EDUCATIONAL ATTAINMENT

		% All House hold Median Income
All-Households	$ 50,971	100%
Less than High School Less than 9th Grade 9-12 Grade	 $ 21,635 $ 25,604	 42.4 50.2
High School Graduate	$ 39,647	77.8
Some College	$ 48,413	95.0
Associate Degree	$ 56,789	111.4
Bachelors Degree	$ 75,518	148.2
Masters Degree	$ 91,660	179.8
Doctorate	$ 120,873	237.1

Source: U.S. Census Bureau, 2009

TRENDS IN CONCENTRATION OF INCOME BY QUINTILE GROUP

	1970	1980	1990	2000	2009
Highest Fifth	43.3%	44.1%	46.6%	49.8%	50.3%
Next Highest Fifth	24.5	24.7	24.0	23.0	23.2
Total	67.8%	68.8%	70.6%	72.8%	73.5%
Middle Fifth	17.4%	16.8%	15.9%	14.8%	14.6%
Next Lowest Fifth	10.8%	10.2%	9.6%	8.9%	8.6%
Lowest Fifth	4.1	4.2	3.8	3.6	3.4

Source: U.S. Census Bureau, Current Population Reports

TRENDS IN SHARE OF AGGREGATE INCOME TOP 5% OF HOUSEHOLDS

1970	16.6%
1980	16.5
1990	18.5
2000	22.1
2009	21.7

Source: U.S. Census Bureau

COMPARATIVE RATIOS HIGHEST INCOME TO LOWEST INCOME HOUSEHOLDS

	Ratio
United States	2.3:1
Germany	2.1:1
United Kingdom	2.0:1
Canada	1.7:1
France	1.5:1
Japan	1.4:1

Source: OECD, 2007. Highest income households comprised of Top 10%; lowest bottom 10%

COUNTRY INCOME INEQUALITY COMPARISONS MEASURED BY GINI INDEX

	Index
United States	45.0
Japan	38.1
United Kingdom	34.0
Switzerland	33.7
France	32.7
Canada	32.1
Australia	30.3
Finland	29.5
Denmark	29.0
Germany	27.0

Source: CIA World Fact Book. The higher the index, the greater the inequality.

B-10

EMPLOYEE COMPENSATION
PERCENTAGE INCREASES vs. PRODUCTIVITY GAINS
(Post Recession Periods)

Period	Compensation	Employee Productivity	Gap
1975 – 79	1.4%	1.4%	+0
1983 – 89	0.2	1.6	(1.4)
1992 – 00	0.1	1.8	(1.7)
2000 – 07	0.0	2.2	(2.2)

Source: Bureau of Labor Statistics/Economic Policy Institute

DECLINE IN U.S. MANUFACTURING EMPLOYMENT
(Millions of Workers)

		% Private Sector Employment
2000	17.3	15.6%
2005	14.2	12.7%
2010	11.6	11.0%

Source: Bureau of Labor Statistics

APPENDIX C

Quality of Life

C-1 U.N. Human Development Index-National Rankings

C-2 The Economist – Quality of Life National Rankings

C-3 Highest Post-Secondary School Enrollment-National Rankings

C-4 Child Well-Being – National Rankings

C-5 Individuals in U.S. Living Below Poverty Level

C-6 Child Poverty Levels By Country

C-7 Educational Attainment of U.S. Persons Aged 25-34

C-8 Proportion of Individuals in the U.S. Without Health Insurance

C-9 National Comparisons of Weeks Worked and Leisure Time

C-1

U.N. HUMAN DEVELOPMENT INDEX NATIONAL RANKINGS

Rank	Country
1	Norway
2	Australia
3	New Zealand
4	United States
5	Ireland
6	Lichtenstein
7	Netherlands
8	Canada
9	Sweden
10	Germany

Source: United Nations, 2010. Based on composite index of health, education and living standards measures

THE ECONOMIST – QUALITY OF LIFE INDEX NATIONAL RANKINGS

Rank	Country
1	Ireland
2	Switzerland
3	Norway
4	Luxembourg
5	Sweden
6	Australia
7	Iceland
8	Italy
9	Denmark
10	Spain
11	Singapore
12	Finland
13	United States

Source: The Economist Intelligence Unit, 2005. Index based on 9 factors: health, family life, community life, material well-being, political stability, climate and geography, job security, political freedom, gender, and equality.

HIGHEST POST-SECONDARY SCHOOL ENROLLMENT NATIONAL BANKINGS

Rank	Country
1	Finland
2	South Korea
3	New Zealand
4	Sweden
5	United States
6	Norway
7	Greece
8	Denmark
9	Latvia
10	Slovenia

Source: The Economist Intelligence Unit, 2005

C-4

CHILD WELL-BEING
NATIONAL RANKINGS

Overall Rank	Material Well-Being	Health/ Safety	Educational Well-Being	Family Friend Relationships
Netherlands	10	2	6	3
Sweden	1	1	5	15
Denmark	4	4	8	9
Finland	3	3	4	17
Spain	12	6	15	8
Switzerland	5	9	14	4
Norway	2	8	11	10
Italy	14	5	20	1
Ireland	19	19	7	7
Belgium	7	16	1	5
United States	17	21	12	20

Source: OECD, 2005

INDIVIDUALS IN U.S. LIVING BELOW POVERTY LEVEL

	Millions	**% Population**
1970	25.4	12.6%
1980	29.3	13.0%
1990	33.6	13.5%
2000	31.6	11.3%
2009	43.5	14.3%

Source: U.S. Census Bureau

CHILD POVERTY LEVELS BY COUNTRY
(% Living in Poverty Households)

United States	21.9%
United Kingdom	15.4
Canada	14.9
Japan	14.3
Germany	10.2
France	7.5
Switzerland	6.8
Sweden	4.2
Norway	3.4
Finland	2.8

Source: OECD, 2005. Percentages based on children in households with income 50% below national median income

EDUCATIONAL ATTAINMENT OF U.S. PERSONS AGED 25-34

Not a High School Graduate	13.0%
High School Graduate	28.6%
Some College	19.1%
Associate Degree	9.3%
Bachelors Degree	21.8%
Advanced Degree	8.1%

Source: U.S. Census Bureau, Current Population Reports, 2006

PERCENTAGE OF INDIVIDUALS IN U.S. WITHOUT HEALTH INSURANCE

All Individuals	**16.8%**
Household Income	
Under $25,000	26.6%
$25,000 - $50,000	21.4
$50,000 - $75,000	16.0
Over $75,000	9.1
Age Group	
Under 18	10.0%
18 – 24	30.4
25 – 34	29.1
35 – 44	21.7
45 – 64	16.1
Over 65	1.8
Racial	
White	15.8%
Black	21.0
Hispanic	32.4
Asian	17.2

Source: U.S. Census Bureau, 2009

NATIONAL COMPARISONS OF WEEKS WORKED AND LEISURE TIME

	Annual Weeks Worked	**Holiday & Vacation Weeks**
United States	46.2	3.9
Switzerland	42.6	6.1
Spain	42.1	7.0
Italy	41.1	7.9
United Kingdom	40.8	6.6
France	40.7	7.0
Germany	40.6	7.8
Netherlands	39.6	7.6
Denmark	39.4	7.4
Finland	38.9	7.1

Source: OECD, 2004

APPENDIX D

Social Safety Nets

D-1 Employee Benefits in the U.S. – Percent Having Access to Benefit

D-2 Low Income Households - Significant U.S. Social Safety Net Programs

D-3 Healthcare – Significant U.S. Social Safety Net Programs

D-4 The Workplace – Significant U.S. Social Safety Net Programs

D-5 Retirement – Significant U.S. Social Safety Net Programs

D-6 Canadian Index of Well-Being – Areas of Measurement

EMPLOYEE BENEFITS IN THE U.S.
PERCENT WORKERS HAVING
ACCESS TO BENEFIT

	Medical Care	**Retirement**	**Sick Leave**	**Vacation**
Private Sector	71%	65%	62%	77%
Full Time	86	74	74	91
Part Time	24	39	26	37
Union	91	88	71	87
Non-Union	68	62	61	76
Wage Level				
Top 25%	92	84	86	89
2nd 25%	86	75	75	89
3rd 25%	76	67	66	84
Lowest 25%	38	40	32	53
Company Size				
1 – 99 Workers	59	51	53	70
100+ Workers	84	81	73	89
500+ Workers	88	85	81	89

Source: U.S. Department of Labor, Bureau of Labor Statistics, March 2010

LOW INCOME HOUSEHOLDS
SIGNIFICANT U.S. SOCIAL
SAFETY NET PROGRAMS

Food Stamps

Began in 1964 as the Supplemental Nutrition Assistance Program. It provides food to low and no-income households. Administered by the U.S. Department of Agriculture.

Head Start

A federal program started in 1965. It provides low income families with early education, health and nutrition services.

Pell Grants

Established in 1965, a federal program created by the Department of Education to provide payments for post secondary education and fees to low income families who qualify on the basis of financial need.

Earned Income Tax Credit (EITC)

A program started in 1975 administered by the Internal Revenue Service for eligible low income families who receive a refundable tax credit with their income tax filing.

HEALTHCARE
SIGNIFICANT U.S. SOCIAL
SAFETY NET PROGRAMS

Medicare

Enacted in 1965. Program provides for federal health insurance coverage for individuals 65 years of age and over and the disabled. Plan covers 80% of medical costs. The balance is the responsibility of individuals or supplemented by private purchase of additional insurance.

Medicaid

Enacted in 1965, a federal-state program providing coverage for individuals with low income or financial resources who qualify on need-based criteria.

State Childrens Health Insurance Program (SCHIP)

Enacted in 1997 as a federal-state program for low income families with children who do not qualify for Medicaid.

Patient Protection and Affordable Care Act

Enacted in 2010, but still subject to court and state challenges. Provides for universal coverage of Americans with a variety of public-private insurance plans.

Veterans Health Administration

A long existing program providing health services to veterans at federally run outpatient clinics, hospitals and nursing homes. Accessibility based on eight level veteran classification rankings.

THE WORKPLACE
SIGNIFICANT U.S. SOCIAL
SAFETY NET PROGRAMS

Fair Labor Standards Act

Enacted in 1938 the Act established a national minimum wage, working hour standards, compensation for overtime and restrictions on the employment of minors. Numerous amendments were made in subsequent years to clarify intent of the law and changes in the workplace environment.

Occupational Safety and Health Administration (OSHA)

Federal agency established in 1970 within the Department of Labor with regulatory authority for making the workplace free of harm to employees, i.e. injury, exposure to toxic chemicals, noise, unsanitary working conditions.

Family Medical Leave Act (FMLA)

Enacted in 1993 requires companies with 50 or more employees to grant up to 12 weeks of unpaid job protected leave to employees for at home care of a child, spouse or elderly family member.

D-5

RETIREMENT
SIGNIFICANT U.S. SOCIAL
SAFETY NET PROGRAMS

Social Security Act of 1935

Established a federal social insurance program funded by employer/employee contributions to be used for making monthly payments to retirees 65 and over. Later amendments included eligible coverage of disabled, surviving spouses and provisions for payment increases tied to raises in the cost of living.

Employment Retirement Security Act of 1974 (ERISA)

Government set new standards for private pension plans. Also created the Pension Benefit Guarantee Corporation, an independent federal agency to insure retirees covered by defined benefit plans against termination, default and company bankruptcy.

Individual Retirement Accounts (IRA)

Allowed individuals to set up independent self-administered retirement accounts and receive a tax deduction for deposits to their account. No taxes would be paid until withdrawal of funds. Plans had limits on amount that could be deposited and these have been revised over time. Later amendments introduced to the basic plans, e.g. Roth IRAs, SEP IRA, Keogh Plans for self-employed workers.

401(k) Plans

These plans were created with a 1978 amendment to the Internal Revenue Code by adding a new 401(k) section effective in 1980. The plans are administered by employers who determine the percentage contribution they want to make or match to an employee's contribution. The plans are now the most dominant of all retiree plans with the exception of the federally funded Social Security Program.

D-6

CANADIAN INDEX OF WELL-BEING AREAS OF MEASUREMENT

Statistical Measures

Living Standards	9
Education	8
Public Health	8
Community	11
Democratic Engagement	8
Time Use	10
Leisure and Culture	8
Environment	TBD

Source: Government of Canada

DATA & STATISTICAL SOURCES

U.S. Government Organizations
U.S. Census Bureau
Congressional Budget Office
U.S. Department of Commerce, Bureau of Economic Analysis
U.S. Department of Defense
U.S. Department of Education, National Center for Education Statistics (NCES)
U.S. Department of Health and Human Services
Internal Revenue Service
U.S. Labor Department, Bureau of Labor Statistics
U.S. Department of Veterans' Affairs

International Organizations
Government of Canada
The European Union
International Labor Organization (ILO)
International Monetary Fund (IMF)
Organization for Economic Cooperation and Development (OECD)
The United Nations Childrens' Fund (UNICEF)
United Nations (UN)
World Bank

World Economic Forum
World Health Organization (WHO)
World Trade Organization (WTO)

Public Policy Advocacy Groups
Center for American Progress
Economic Policy Institute
Kaiser Family Foundation
Pension Rights Center
Progressive Policy Institute
Urban Institute

Other Sources
American Federation of Labor – Congress of Industrial Organizations (AFL-CIO)
Center for Retirement Research at Boston College
The College Board
Economist Intelligence Unit
Employee Benefit Research Institute (EBRI)
Investment Company Institute
MetLife
The New York Times
Pew Research Center for the People and the Press
Statistical Abstract of the United States
The Wall Street Journal
Wikipedia

BIBLIOGRAPHY

Adams, James Truswell. *The Epic of America.* Simon Publications, 2001.

Bacevich, Andrew J. *Washington Rules. America's Path to Permanent War.* Henry Holt & Company, 2010.

Bernstein, Peter L. *Against the Gods: The Remarkable Story of Risk.* Wiley, 1999.

Bok, Derek. *The Politics of Happiness: What Government Can Learn from the New Research or Well-Being.* Princeton University Press, 2010.

Boorstin, Daniel J. *The Americans: The Colonial Experience.* Random House, 1958.

Bowman, John S. *The Cambridge Dictionary of American Biography.* Cambridge University Press, 1995.

Boyer, Paul S. (ed.). *Oxford Companion to United States History.* Oxford University Press, 2001.

Brands, H.W. *American Dreams: The United States Since 1945.* Penguin Press, 2010.

Brooks, Arthur S. *Gross National Happiness.* Basic Books, 2008.

Cullen, Jim. *The American Dream: A Short History of an Idea that Shaped the Nation.* Oxford University Press, 2004.

Delbanco, Andrew. *The Real American Dream: A Meditation on Hope.* Harvard University Press, 2000.

Esterbrook, Greg. *The Progress Paradox: How Life Gets Better While People Feel Worse.* Random House, 2004.

Ford, Martin. *The Lights in the Tunnel: Automated Technology and the Economy of the Future.* Createspace, 2009.

Forner, Eric, and John A. Garelty (eds.). *Readers Companion to American History.* Houghton Mifflin Company, 1993.

Frank, Robert H. *Falling Behind: How Rising Inequality Harms the Middle Class.* University of California Press, 1997.

Frank, Robert H. and Phillip Cook. *The Winner Take All Society: Why the Few at the Top Get So Much More Than the Rest of Us.* Penguin, 1996.

Franklin, Benjamin. *Poor Richard's Almanac.* Skyhorse Publishing, 2007.

Garraty, John A., Sternstein, Jerome L. (eds.), 2nd Edition. *Encyclopedia of American Biography: In-Depth Profiles of Over 1,000 Prominent Americans.* Harper Collins, 1996.

Gosselin, Peter. *High Wire: The Precarious Financial Lives of American Families* Basic Books, 2008.

Graham, Carol. *Happiness Around the World: The Paradox of Happy Peasants and Miserable Millionaires.* Oxford University Press, 2010.

Greenhouse, Steven. *The Big Squeeze: Tough Times for the American Worker.* Alfred A. Knopf, 2008.

Hacker, Jacob S. *The Great Risk Shift: The New Economic Insecurity and the Decline of the American Dream.* Oxford University Press, 2008.

Handlin, Oscar. *The Uprooted: The Epic Story of the Great Migrations That Made the American People.* Little, Brown and Company, 1973.

Harrison, Lawrence E. and Samuel P. Huntington. *Culture Matters: How Values Share Human Progress.* Basic Books, 2000.

Hill, Steven. *Europe's Promise: Why the European Way is the Best Hope in an Industrial Age.* University of California Press, 2010.

Huffington, Ariana. *Third World Americans: How Our Politicians Are Abandoning the Middle Class and Betraying the American Dream.* Crowne, 2010.

Huntington, Samuel P. *Who We Are: The Challenges to America's National Identity.* Simon & Schuster, 2004.

Humes Edward. *Over Here: How the GI Bill Transformed the American Dream.* Houghton Mifflin Harcourt, 2006.

Johnson, Paul. *A History of the American People.* Harper Perennial, 1999.

Landes, David S. *The Wealth and Poverty of Nations: Why Some Are So Rich and Some Are So Poor.* WW Norton & Company, 1998.

Le Blanc, Paul. *A Short History of the U.S. Working Class.* Humanity Books, 1999.

Lewis, Richard D. *Finland: Cultural Lone Wolf.* Intercultural Press, 2004.

Lipset, Seymour. *American Exceptionalism: A Double Edged Sword.* Norton, 1996.

Meacham, Jon. *American Lion: Andrew Jackson in the White House.* Random House Trade Paperbacks, 2009.

Merk, Fredrick. *History of the Westward Movement.* Alfred A. Knopf, 1978.

Mishele, Bernstein, Shierholz. *The State of Working America, 2008/2009.* Cornell University Press, 2009.

Morgan, Edmund S. *The Puritan Dilemma: The Story of John Winthrop.* Longman, 2006.

Moss, David A. *When All Else Fails: Government as the Ultimate Risk Manager,* Harvard University Press, 2004.

Parini, Jay. (ed.). *The Norton Book of American Biography.* W.W. Norton & Co. 1999.

Patterson, James T. *Grand Expectations: The United States 1945-1974.* Oxford University Press, 1997.

Reich, Robert B. *Aftershock: The Next Economy and America's Future.* Knopf, 2010.

Rifkin, Jeremy. *The European Dream: How Europe's Vision of the Future is Eclipsing The American Dream.* Penguin, 2004.

_____. *The End of Work.* Penguin Putnam, 1995.

Samuelson, Robert S. *The Good Life and Its Discontents: The American Dream in the Age of Entitlement.* Vintage, 1997.

Schlesinger, Jr., Arthur M. *The Cycles of American History.* Mariner Books, 1999.

_____. *The Age of Jackson.* Back Bay Books, 1988.

Stiglitz, Joseph E. *Free Fall: America, Free Markets and the Sinking of the World Economy.* W. W. Norton & Company, 2010.

_____. *Globalization and Its Discontents.* W.W. Norton & Company, 2003.

_____. *Roaring Nineties: A New History of the World's Most Prosperous Decade.* W.W. Norton & Company, 2004.

Tocqueville, Alexis de. *Democracy in America.* Harper Perennial Modern Classics, 2006.

Turner, Fredrick Jackson. *The Frontier in American History.* Biblio Bazzar, 2008.

Uchitelle, Louis. *The Disposable American: Layoffs and Their Consequences.* Vintage, 2007.

Weber, Max. *The Protestant Ethic and the Spirit of Capitalism.* Scribners, 1953.

Whyte, William H. *The Organization Man.* Doubleday, 1956.

Wills, Gary. *Inventing America: Jefferson's Declaration of Independence.* Mariner Books, 2002.

Zinn, Howard. *A People's History of the United States.* Harper Perennial Modern Classics, 2010.

ACKNOWLEDGEMENTS

It was not too many years ago that an author's acknowledgements largely cited people interviewed, places visited, libraries, and research assistants who tediously tracked down the sources of information needed to write one's book. Today, in an electronic age, a good deal of this has now changed.

The Internet can, and did provide much of the source material for this book – innumerable data bases, government files and documents, university research studies, speeches, news reports and more. Public libraries today also provide readily accessible resources that were not available just a few years ago – comprehensive online catalogs, electronic ordering and book delivery systems. I was able to draw extensively on the Miami-Dade County Public library system, with their 3.5 million volumes and more than 150 online databases.

A list is provided of the major data and statistical sources used in the preparation of this book, together with a four-part 30-table appendix and a bibliography. Rather than individual footnote references in the body of the text, sources are cited directly or are available in these supporting materials.

As for people to whom I owe gratitude, these go largely to mentions of my family – my son, Jeffrey, a copywriter, whose suggestions helped enhance the book's readability; my son-in-law, Mike Manzi, an inquisitive reader of American history, who gave me important feedback on whether or not the various sections of the book would be understandable and of interest to everyday readers. And, finally, my wife, Barbara, who not only also did what both Jeffrey and Mike did, but had the burden of typing the manuscript. Yes, in this electronic age a lot can be replaced, but not people who are important to us.

Made in the USA
Charleston, SC
21 September 2011